SIT TIGHT, AND I'LL SWING
YOU A TAIL . . .

SIT TIGHT, AND I'LL SWING YOU A TAIL . . .

*Using and Writing Stories
with Young People*

GREGORY A. DENMAN

*Heinemann
Portsmouth, NH*

Heinemann Educational Books, Inc.
361 Hanover Street
Portsmouth, NH 03801-3959
Offices and agents throughout the world

Acknowledgments begin on page ix.

Library of Congress Cataloging-in-Publication Data
Denman, Gregory A.
    Sit tight, and I'll swing you a tail— : using and writing stories
with young people / Gregory A. Denman.
        p.   cm.
    Includes bibliographical references and index.
    ISBN 0-435-08548-4
    1. Storytelling—United States.   2. Language arts (Elementary)
I. Title.
LB1042.D46   1991
372.6'42—dc20   91-271
                                                                  CIP

Front- and back-cover photographs by Wendell Bull Photos.
Figures by Michael E. Cellan (except where otherwise noted).
Designed by Wladislaw Finne.
Printed in the United States of America.
91   92   93   94   95   9   8   7   6   5   4   3   2   1

*To the writers and tellers
who create stories—*

*the students
who delight in them—*

*and the teachers
who lovingly bring
the two together.*

CONTENTS

ACKNOWLEDGMENTS

The following have generously given permission to use quotations from copyrighted works:

Pages 10–11: From *Storytelling: Process and Practice* by Norma J. Livo and Sandra A. Rietz. Littleton, CO: Libraries Unlimited, 1986. Reprinted by permission.

Page 21: From *Sam, Bangs and Moonshine* by Evaline Ness. Copyright © 1966 by Evaline Ness. Published by Henry Holt and Company, Inc. Reprinted by permission.

Page 24: Reprinted by permission of Atheneum Publishers, an imprint of Macmillan Publishing Company from *Shadow of a Bull* by Maia Wojciechowska. Copyright © 1964 Maia Wojciechowska.

Pages 71, 72: From *Millions of Cats* by Wanda Gág. Copyright © 1928 by Coward-McCann, Inc., copyright renewed © 1956 by Robert Janssen. Reprinted by permission.

Page 101: From *Tikki Tikki Tembo* retold by Arlene Mosel. Copyright © 1968 by Arlene Mosel. Published by Henry Holt and Company, Inc. Reprinted by permission.

Every effort has been made to contact copyright holders for permission to reprint borrowed material. We regret any oversights that may have occurred and would be happy to rectify them in future printings of this work.

ABOUT THIS BOOK

One might think that my dear parents are confused.

Recently, when asked what I do for a living, my mother responded quickly, with an obvious hint of maternal pride in her voice, "Why, he's a writer and language arts consultant!" My dad looked at her, duly rolling his eyes, with the same expression he wears whenever she overglorifies one of her children. "Honey, he's a 'storyteller.' " As always, they are both right.

Yes, Mom, I am a writer and language arts consultant (aren't we all consultants about something these days?). And yes, Dad, I am a modern-day version of a "teller of tales." Both hats seem to fit comfortably. Those familiar with *When You've Made It Your Own . . . Teaching Poetry to Young People* may recall that I spend a good portion of my time conducting workshops and classes on poetry and storytelling for teachers. But I also teach language arts methods to undergraduate education students and children's literature to graduate students. While this may make me appear quite the academician, don't be fooled! Some days find me in a school somewhere, happily seated on a frayed carpet telling stories to a group of first graders. I am one of many traveling storytellers hired by schools, churches, and conferences to entertain audiences with stories. Perhaps some of you have had the opportunity to see and hear a few of the fine professional storytellers currently working in this way.

This book allows me to wear both hats at the same time. As a storyteller, I compose and develop stories to use in my performances. To do so I have studied a broad range of topics—the art of storytelling, folklore, the folktale, oral tradition—which I draw on to devise strategies for helping young people read, write, and tell stories more joyfully and more proficiently. Many of the approaches I describe in this book were conceived and refined during my ten years as an elementary school teacher.

Others have been developed more recently through the artist-in-residence programs in which I have participated in a number of states as a visiting storyteller or poet. Still others have been gleaned from professional reading and research and from conference presentations of current theory. This book, then, is intended as a demonstration of all of these—a melting pot of theory and application, of method and practice, of idea and implementation, and of artist and teacher. I hope that *Sit Tight, and I'll Swing You a Tail . . .* shows where the teller and the teacher connect in the classroom and become one. Using stories in a way that excites children's imaginations and sets the stage for a life full of literary adventures must be one of our most important educational objectives. It has assuredly been reward enough for me.

A brief warning: if you want a book on how to become a storyteller or on how to write and perform stories, this is not the book for you. There are fine materials now on the market that provide this kind of information. If you are looking for an in-depth study of folklore or of oral tradition, you will have to seek out other sources. If you need a comprehensive reading/writing/language arts text, sorry again; I make no claims to having even adequately covered these topics. What I want to share here is a written version of my work: the stories and techniques I use with children and teachers in my day-to-day activities as a storyteller and a teacher. So,

> *Take what you can use,*
> *Adapt it if you need to,*
> *Discard what doesn't ring true.*

ONE

STORIES

STORIES AND STORYTELLING

We are a storying people.

In present-day South Africa, an aged black woman sits comfortably on the ground, her head swaddled in a cotton turban to protect her from the glare of the noonday sun. Surrounding her, propped between clasped hands, are the wide-eyed faces of the Xhosa children. The woman is relating a narrative of her people called a *ntsomi*. As she speaks, her hands dance in front of her like agile marionettes, suggesting the action of her words. The Xhosa children listen intently, their eyes never breaking contact with the storyteller. As tribal tradition dictates, it will be the children's turn to tell the *ntsomi* when they become parents and grandparents (Pellowski 1977, 47).

Along the Ivory Coast, many miles from the fields inhabited by the Xhosa people, an ancient maxim claims that the *gouros* gods will give children only to those who can tell at least a hundred tales. Children of the Ewe People of Ghana are not considered educated unless they have learned the *gliwo*, a series of animal stories that teach basic lessons in obedience, kindness, courage, honesty, and other virtues (Pellowski 1977, 45).

In Japan, a popular form of storytelling called *Kamishibai* or "theater of paper" has evolved (Pellowski 1977, 144). Performances of these stories, presented in streets and squares are accompanied by picture cards held in wooden frames. The storytellers, who often

1

maintain a repertoire of three or four stories, usually travel the Japanese countryside on bicycles, selling candy to children between performances.

Each fall in Jonesborough, Tennessee, thousands of people gather in huge circus tents to hear nationally and internationally renowned storytellers. For three full days, these modern masters of the craft delight audiences with every imaginable type of tale. In between sessions, people swap tales of their own and buy and sell cassette tapes of recorded stories.

Storytelling, an art form far older than recorded history, is bounded neither by continent, nor by culture. Stories are found whenever and wherever human beings gather. As Ruth Sawyer describes it in *The Way of the Storyteller,* storytelling is "a folk art that has grown out of the primal urge to give tongue to what has been seen, heard or experienced" (Sawyer 1970, 5). Whether the story is a historical legend, a religious or moral tale, or a contemporary anecdote, humankind has historically yearned to hear the storyteller's words:

> In the villages of central Africa, in outrigger boats on the Pacific, in the Australian bush, and within the shadow of Hawaiian volcanoes, tales of the present and of the mysterious past, of animals and gods and heroes, and of men and women like themselves, hold listeners in their spell or enrich the conversation of daily life. So it is also in Eskimo igloos under the light of seal-oil lamps, in the tropical jungles of Brazil, and by the totem poles of the British Columbian coast. In Japan too, and China and India, the priest and the scholar, the peasant and the artisan all join in their love of a good story and their honor for the man who tells it well. (Thompson 1977, 3)

Stories are the warp on which the fabric of our cultural history has been woven. They have a magical ability to connect us to the past and to those who came before us. A collection of Egyptian tales on papyrus known as the *Tales of the Magicians* dates back as far as 4000 B.C. The tales begin with an encounter between the king, Khufu, and his sons:

> Know ye a man who can tell me tales of the deeds of magicians? Then the royal son Khafra stood forth and said, "I will tell thy Majesty a tale of the days of thy forefather." (Pellowski 1977, 4)

This device, grouping stories together around a central idea, was repeated two or three thousand years later in *The Thousand and One Arabian Nights*. Boccaccio used the same technique in the *Decameron*, as did Chaucer in the *Canterbury Tales*. The brilliant, contemporary storyteller Jay O'Callahan recently presented to audiences across the United States a series of stories centered around the little—at times, unnoticed—things people do that make them heroic. He called his stories "Village Heroes."

Storytelling has deep roots in our cultural past. Classical sources demonstrate the prevalence of storytelling in ancient Greece. In Euripides' play *Heracles,* written in 425 B.C., Amphitryon says:

> *Be calm*
> *dry the living springs of tears that fill*
> *your children's eyes. Console them*
> *with stories,*
> *those sweet thieves of wretched*
> *make-believe.*
> (PELLOWSKI 1977, 5)

Aristophanes' *Lysistrata* (ca. 415 B.C.) also contains a reference to storytelling:

> *I want to tell you a fable*
> *they used to relate to me*
> *when I was a little boy.*
> (PELLOWSKI 1977, 5)

The Middle Ages, as Ruth Sawyer states, were a "time of rich harvest for those who had the wit to create, the memory to hold and the grace of tongue to recount tales that could amuse" (Sawyer 1945, 69–70). This period saw the development of the bawdy story along with numerous legends of Christ, the Virgin, and the saints. Stories that at one time enchanted one people, one culture, often travel to another locale at a later time. Retold and transformed, like a piece of music recast by a conductor for a new performance, stories have moved over continents and across oceans. In the life course of a story, a detail may be forgotten, the age or sex of a character may be altered, or the order of events may be rearranged, but the story remains. The familiar fairy tales of Perrault or the Brothers Grimm are examples of stories that have been preserved through the centuries on the tongues of storytellers and, more recently, through the pens of writers and illustrators.

Stories function on many different levels and serve many purposes: to entertain, to educate, to give information, to explain a historical reference, to showcase ethnic characteristics. The list could go on, but not least would be the role of stories in helping individuals gain a healthy sense of themselves and their lives. In his article, "A Note on Story," James Hilton argues that to have been exposed to stories in childhood helps a person "integrate life as story," because one has stories in the back of the mind that act as containers for organizing events into meaningful experiences. This may be crucial for psychological wholeness in later life (Hilton 1979, 43).

In the same vein, Bruno Bettelheim states in his popular and sometimes provocative book, *The Uses of Enchantment,* that "stories train kids to predict outcomes, possibly the outcome of their own behavior." In this way, stories, and fairy tales in particular, become rehearsals for adulthood.

> Each fairy tale is a magic mirror which reflects some aspects of
> our inner world, and of the steps required by our evolution
> from immaturity to maturity. For those who immerse
> themselves in what the fairy tale has to communicate, it
> becomes a deep, quiet pool which at first seems to reflect only
> our own image; but behind it we soon discover the inner
> turmoils of our soul—its depth, and ways to gain peace within
> ourselves and with the world, which is the reward of our
> struggles. (Bettelheim 1975, 309)

Stories are lenses through which we view and review all of human experience. No other being on earth can create stories. They have a power to reach deep inside us and command our ardent attention. Through stories we see ourselves. Our individual follies, misgivings, and triumphs become part of humankind's follies, misgivings, and triumphs. Our personal existence, however trivial it may seem, takes on a cloak of significance. Through stories, we see what it is to be alive, to be human.

STORIES IN THE CLASSROOM

The past twenty years have witnessed something of an explosion of interest in storytelling in the United States. Prior to 1960, storytelling was chiefly perceived picture book "story times" in libraries. In the years since, talented professional storytellers have been emerging all over the country. The National Association for the Preservation and Perpetuation of Storytelling (NAPPS) based in Jonesborough, Tennessee, boasts a membership of thirty-five hundred and maintains a catalog of two hundred and fifty active "professional storytellers" and storytelling groups. And this figure does not take into account the thousands of librarians, teachers, and other folks from all walks of life who tell stories for fun.

Some tellers write or develop their own materials. Others are "traditionalists" who tell stories they have heard firsthand; regional, ethnic, or family stories often come from these types of tellers. Still other storytellers gather their materials from literary sources such as children's literature and adult literary stories. Some work in tandem with other tellers; others are members of storytelling ensemble groups. Some incorporate music and dance into their tales, while others use mime or sign language. The field of storytelling is rich with limitless possibilities of form and presentation. Indeed, children and adults alike have many opportunities to experience a well-told story today.

My own beginnings as a storyteller can be traced back to a rather unpretentious corner of a third-grade classroom in Manitou Springs, Colorado. I was two or three years into my teaching career and had begun to hear of this thing called "storytelling." Stories, picture books, and poems had always been a lively part of my classroom. My third graders had frequently been read the story of Alexander and his very bad day; had heard many times over everything Maurice Sendak has written; had listened to the entire cycle of Roald Dahl books; had enjoyed repeated readings of the Bill Peet word masterpieces; and had cried through the touching moments of Peck's *A Day No Pigs Would Die* and Rawls's *Summer of the Monkeys* and *Where the Red Fern Grows*. We had also written and illustrated our own picture books, adapted children's stories for a series of readers' theater performances, and started a school literary journal. In telling stories, I was quite simply a teacher, not an actor.

I did, however, have a couple of encouraging models. My undergraduate language arts professor had been a master storyteller with picture books, and a friend of mine was starting to acquire a reputation as a local storyteller. It was not long before my wife had to weather repeated practice sessions of one story or another. Finally one day, without much fanfare, I gathered my third graders for story time. "How 'bout I tell you a story today, kids? I've got some notes here in case I forget a part." That was the shaky premier of my first telling of Rudyard Kipling's *The Elephant's Child.*

It still astonishes me how far one can go with little knowledge and even less talent. They liked it! So did the second graders the following day—and other groups of young people eight years later when I launched my career as a "professional" storyteller and language arts consultant. I will always remember the delight of discovering the difference between reading a story and telling one. When I read a story out loud, I am tied to the print, locked to the page. There is a persistent "Jiminy Cricket" stab of conscience saying, "Follow word for word. Stick to what's written, buddy." But when I tell a story, my version can be as free as my unburdened hands and eyes. When my memory fails me, my imagination charges in to take over. And I can enjoy my rendition of a story along with my listeners. In those early days, as my fondness for telling grew, so did my repertoire. Although I continued to read to my class, "told stories" became a frequent special addition to our story time.

Whether they hear a story from a professional storyteller, a storytelling teacher, or simply a teacher who reads aloud, students gain immensely from listening to a wide variety of stories. The benefits extend well beyond entertainment. Listening to stories encourages the growth of children's natural love of language and verbal expression. It serves as a vital link in the acquisition of language, for both reading and writing.

My research and experience bear witness to the fact that, from their earliest years, children listen, and listen intently. During the preschool and primary school years, children's imaginations and their ability to visualize are unhampered by a rigid sense of reality. They are free to delight in the mere sound of words and the way sounds blend together as they roll off the storyteller's or reader's tongue. They are also free to surrender themselves to the rhythm of words and sentences. Holding in mind the rhythm of a poem or tune or story helps children focus their thoughts, which theorists maintain is the foundation for a well-developed imaginative and intellectual life in adulthood.

Bill Martin Jr, author and editor of the Sounds of Language reading series, stresses that each of us has a "linguistic storehouse" in which we "deposit" stories, poems, sentences, and words. Their patterns, which enter through the ear, remain available to our reading, writing, and speaking throughout our lives. Martin maintains that even children with a seemingly meager vocabulary can latch onto the structure or patterns of language they hear. Suddenly, children find their own "vocabulary taking on new strength" (Martin and Brogan 1972).

Hearing a variety of good stories can also serve to expand children's reading interests. When they get into a "reading rut," continually seeking out the same story or story type, a storytelling teacher can give them examples of other kinds of written materials and gradually lead them into reading in other fields and subjects. The teacher's enthusiasm gives the reluctant child the impression that stories and reading are worth the effort. Reading then becomes a natural and enviable activity for every child, lending credence to Don Holdaway's statement that "learning to read and to write ought to be one of the most joyful and successful of human undertakings" (Holdaway 1979, 11).

Research in reading has highlighted the gap between children's reading and their capacity to understand and enjoy literature at a higher level. Independent reading ability often lags behind listening comprehension by many years. But stories, told or read, require no ability grouping. A four- or six-year-old can fully experience a story he or she may not yet be able to read. If the action is clear and the plot consistent with the listener's idea of what a story is, the storyteller can use mature, complex language. Strange words and uncommon pronunciations will not bewilder the child.

Children's minds delight in hearing unusual words and sentences. They love language for its own sake; they treasure words almost as they do friends. My third graders have for years repeated Kipling's alliterative gem from my first storytelling attempt: "go to the banks of the great grey-green greasy Limpopo River." The words children hear while listening to a good story are easier for them to recognize and learn in print afterward. Their speaking vocabulary increases and their ears become trained to the music of language. Their feeling for the beauty and power of words grows. The philosopher Jean-Paul Sartre claimed that he learned to read by taking a little book to bed each night, one that had been read aloud to him so often he knew it by heart, and looking at the words as he repeated the "little dried voices" he heard in his head.

Hearing stories during the course of their school life can strengthen children's creative impulses, particularly in the area of writing. Through stories, children become aware of how figurative language is used, by "role-playing" as writers they can try out this literary language. Enjoying a well-told story involves more than merely liking it. To enjoy a story is to be stimulated by the words and brought to new insights and linguistic perceptions. As Bettelheim has said, "through stories children gain access to the richness in their own minds."

Finally, storytelling and reading aloud expand and enhance the young child's exposure to literature. Through stories, students claim a bit of their literary heritage, for all children—regardless of their economic status—are born into a world of stories, a world filled with pleasure or the possibility of pleasures yet to be experienced. Whatever their tone or theme, stories reach out to listeners, reassuring them, reducing their alienation, and bringing a sense of belonging. Beginning readers are not yet capable of truly reading literature. They are far too busy decoding words and sounds to pay attention to its aesthetic value or to experience its emotional satisfactions. But when they listen to a story they can feel the warmth of the storyteller's or reader's affection for the material. Hearing the rhythm of the words, children can experience a sense of the ways in which literature brings us into closer contact with the rest of humanity. It is this same response that will bring these children back to literature as readers later in life. What the eyes cannot yet decipher, the ears and heart can absorb. As James Stephens said so well, "What the heart knows today the head will understand tomorrow."

THE STORY CIRCLE

Ah, the story circle!

I can remember always dreading the required beginning-of-the-year explanations: line up this way, hang coats here, set math texts here on the shelf, store lunchboxes in the corner by the ball box. There were classroom rules, playground rules, rules for the lunchroom and for the halls. There were lists of things to remember: Who goes to special reading? Who visits the counselor every Thursday? Only toward the end of that first day could I relax and say, "Now that we know and understand our rules and procedures, why don't we gather together in the story circle for a story?" All the mechanics of classroom management would fade away as I began reading the book I had chosen. Picture it: a special place, a storybook, and a group of children embarking on a new year.

There was always a kind of mental transformation in the children as they gathered in the area I designated the "story circle." They would leave the hard reality of their endless academic tasks, of worksheets that would eventually demonstrate accomplishment and failure, and come together to be transported in mind and spirit—to a place where dragons were real or three wishes were granted to a deserving soul. In this place, realistic and enchanted characters alike moved about freely, unhampered by what was possible and what was not. For the children it was close to what we as adults experience when we are truly engrossed in a good novel—total abandonment to the reality of the story at hand.

When I was writing my book on poetry, I had to focus all my reading time on textbooks, including books on poetry, books about reading instruction, and books expounding theories of literature. But when the manuscript was finally completed, I treated myself to the luxury of a novel: Unplugging my telephone, I spent an entire weekend completely lost in the lives of a fictional family, watching them, going where they went, worrying about them, and finally celebrating their triumphs.

It is this absorption, an almost trancelike response to a story, that Samuel Taylor Coleridge called the "willing suspension of disbelief." The literature on storytelling abounds with accounts of audiences under the spell of a good story. Some writers have even called this conscious abandonment a "story's witchery," but whether it is witchery or just plain escapism, it makes reading or listening to a story a precious time, a gift to the soul. Freed from the ordinary and the mundane we join, if temporarily, a fictional world. Although research indicates that the human brain has a special affinity to story and story form, the ability to respond to stories is a nurtured behavior learned primarily through human contact. It may begin with the infant cradled in a parent's arms or the young child sitting on a lap or tucked under covers listening to a bedtime story. It should certainly continue in the classroom with a sensitive and enthusiastic teacher and piles of wonderful books.

The recent popularity of "Big Books"—oversized books primary-grade teachers use with groups of youngsters in the classroom—is based on the principle that children can learn to read and respond to print when the situation in which they encounter books mimics the experience of a bedtime story. Don Holdaway, a professor of reading in Australia who conceived what is now referred to as the "shared book experience," wanted to introduce children to reading and books while bypassing the more traditional approach of learning the sounds and sight words first. In a shared book experience, children gather around a teacher with a Big Book, which they read and reread together. Using Big Books encourages what theorists call a "neurological impress," because children actively participate by reading along with the teacher. This approach further supports what I believe we have always intuitively known: that reading is learned by engaging in reading and that learning to read is actually a very natural act for most children.

Just as the young child has special places for coming to stories (the bed or a parent's lap or the rocking chair), in the classroom, too, there should be a special place for this type of interaction.

When I was teaching, my desk seemed too authoritarian and too distant from my listeners, but there was always an intimate corner I could designate as the "story circle" where the children could come to hear stories. Now, as a professional storyteller, one of the first things I ask when I enter the classroom is where the teacher reads to the class. If a child responds, "Oh, let's see, he always sits in the comfortable, green chair in the corner, and we sit on the floor around him," then I know the group will probably be good listeners, ready to interact with my stories. But if the child hems and haws, "Hmm . . . let's see, he sits sometimes at his desk, but mostly he doesn't read to us," then I figure I have my work as a storyteller cut out for me. Establishing a specific place and a regular time for story sharing in the classroom—much as with the time-honored bedtime story—creates a pleasurable sense of ritual and expectation. Often that expectation is to be comfortably transported to another dimension of reality—the reality of the story. For many years Rod Serling signalled this transition to television audiences with the phrase, "You are entering the Twilight Zone."

Storytellers in the oral tradition have always used rituals to convey this sense of being transported to a timeless place. Historically, these story customs and rituals are tied in with the teller's culture: Hopi Indians burned sage before a storytelling session, for example, and tribal groups in Africa might dance and chant. Often, storytellers had a verbal "opening" ritual in which the audience would partic- ipate. In *Storytelling: Practice and Process,* Norma Livo and Sandra Rietz, describe this process:

> The storytelling is initiated by ritual (liturgy or protocol) that announces a shift of realities—from this time to the "other" or "story" time, from today's truth to "story" truth. The participants "cross over" into the place where the stories happen and where they are personally safe from both story and real-life consequences. Many traditional storytellers lead the audience into the game by "calling them over." Using conventions not unlike game-signaling calls such as "Olley olley oxenfree!" the storyteller must enter game space and time first, then "pull" the audience in. To do this, the teller assumes the role of "other." The teller is no longer himself or herself, but the timeless one or the ancient one—the one of the stories. Then the teller calls the audience, or pulls them into the game. One call-response ritual opening for storytellings actually names the phenomenon of crossing over, and the audience asks the teller to pull them in.

Storyteller:	Let's tell another story.
	Let's be off!
Audience:	Pull away!
Storyteller:	Let's be off!
Audience:	Pull away!

(ORIGIN UNKNOWN)

Additional response-call openings were:

Storyteller:	Cric!
Audience:	Crac!

(WEST INDIES)

Storyteller:	Hello . . .
Audience:	Helloooooooooo . . .

(WEST AFRICA)

Storyteller:	A story, a story.
Audience:	Let it come. Let it go.

(WEST AFRICA)
(Livo and Rietz 1986, 12–13)

In the classroom, a similar ritual atmosphere can be created in the story circle. With my third graders I used a "magic candle." I told them that I had received it from a wizard who said that whenever the candle was lit, all within view of its flame would "see and believe all they heard" (the third-grade version of "suspension of disbelief"). As part of our ritual, we would hang a sign on our door that read: STORY TIME—PLEASE DO NOT DISTURB. We would gather in the story circle, turn out the lights, and light the candle. Then we would listen to the story. At the end of our story, we ceremoniously blew out the candle, turned on the lights, and took down our sign. As a group we returned to the land of reality, of "consequence."

A fixture in the story circle was a wooden bar stool (cut down to child size) we called the *story stool*. Throughout the year, this stool was the platform from which I read or told stories, or from which students read stories they had written. I always remember the fall I left the third grade to teach fifth grade and was setting up my new classroom. I assumed that the sophisticated fifth graders would scoff at the candle and the stool, so I was more than gratified to hear the first thing those fifth graders asked: "Still got the magic candle and the story stool?"

A number of other storytelling rituals work equally well:

- Primary teachers may have large stuffed animals as "story partners." The animals introduce the story each day and remind the children of good listening habits. Each day a selected child gets to hold the "story partner" during the story.
- Some kindergarten teachers use an imaginary rope wrapped around the arms of the students. They form a circle and the teacher lets each child hold a section of the imaginary rope. Then they all set the rope on the ground, creating a kind of fairy ring. Before they may step into the fairy ring, the children must be prepared to "see and believe" all they hear.
- A storytelling friend of mine has a wraparound skirt with large pockets for books. The children gather on the floor and select a pocket (and its book) for the session.
- One year, a student teacher of mine made a story vest for me with pictures of story characters sewn on to it. When I put on the vest, I was magically transformed: I became the "storyteller."
- When I was still teaching in the regular classroom, the principal would take my class so I could tell stories to children in the other grades. The ritual I created was the *story hat* (an old hat of mine the children could easily recognize). On the morning of the day I was to visit another class, I would leave the hat on the teacher's desk. Then, when I arrived, I would pick up the hat and put it on my head, and the children would know that they should gather for a story. Holding out the hat like a bowl, I would allow one child to reach in and pull out an imaginary story title and hand it to me. "Why, this is the tale of 'The Three Pigs' "—and we would begin.

The ritual and regularity of the time-honored story circle may be the saving grace of our modern classrooms. As we surge ahead into the high-tech world of the nineties, where computers and specialized instructional programs dominate, the story circle may be the last vestige of the homelike atmosphere that characterized the slower paced classrooms of two or three generations ago. It may become the one place where every student is lovingly accepted regardless of skill level or proficiency. It may be the one time during the day when something is given freely without "educational objective or task-mandated" strings attached. It will surely be the one form of interaction between teacher and student in which mutual affection is nearly guaranteed.

A STORY'S HEART

Once . . .
Once upon a time . . .
Long ago . . .
There were formerly a king and a queen . . .
In a time quite distant from our own . . .
A soldier there was once . . .
In the high and far-off time . . .
Soon upon a time and not so far ahead . . .

So a story begins and in due course ends:

. . . and that's the end of that.
. . . so it is to this day.
. . . they lived happily ever after.
. . . and that's the story of———.
. . . snip snap snout,
  this tale's told out.

In between the "once" and the "ever after" lies the heart of a story—the pearl of significance encased by the story's body. We take this pearl into our own experience, and it becomes part of our reservoir of human understanding—the unspoken knowledge we can rely on and call on throughout our lives. Referring to fantasy, the writer Jane Yolen perhaps expresses this phenomenon best: "Fantasy speaks many times to the listener. Once in the ear, and again, and again, etc., in the echo chamber that is heart" (Yolen 1981, 67). How then do we encourage children to go beyond passive listening to true hearing, to move from mere word decoding to experiential reading? Here is an exercise I have used with children.

First, I have them draw a square on a piece of art paper:

This is the box of reality—
how things really are in life.
Hard Core Actuality! If your
parents ask you what you've been
up to, it's from this box that you
should supply your answer.

Then, I have them draw a circle a short distance to the side of the square:

This is the circle of Truth, something
deeper than the actuality of the moment,

something implied about similar moments.
We'll talk more about this later.

Finally, I have them draw a bridge from the box to the circle and a path leaving the circle returning to the box. (See Figure 1–1.) "Now," I tell them, "I am going to tell you the story of Owl."

[Story summary:] Owl thinks he is ugly. One evening he meets a girl and, in the darkness, they begin to like each other. But, Owl believes that if it were light and the girl could see his face, she would never like him. After many evening visits, Owl and the girl decide to get married, but the girl's mother questions why it is only during the evening that Owl visits. They decide to have a party for Owl on a Sunday afternoon. Owl is nervous, so he decides to ask his cousin Rooster to accompany him. While riding their horses to the party, Owl notices how elegant and proud Rooster is compared to him. He eventually tells Rooster to go to the party without him and to explain that he had an accident and will try to come later. Rooster goes to the party, and after the sun sets, Owl arrives wearing a hat pulled down over his face. He has Rooster explain that a branch scratched his eyes and that any light would hurt them. The girl is happy to see Owl, even with his hat, and invites him to dance. Owl begins dancing and

Figure 1–1 The Story Cycle

enjoying the party. He pulls Rooster off to the side, asking that he warn him by crowing when the sun comes up, so that he can leave before anyone sees his face. In the excitement of the party, the sun slowly creeps up until there is enough light to see by. At the moment Rooster crows, the mother pulls the hat from Owl's face. Owl cries out and runs out of the house, covering his face with his hands. The girl follows, and when Owl takes down his hands to get on his horse, the girl sees his face. It is the most handsome face she has ever seen. But Owl rides off, never to return. The girl eventually marries Rooster. (Wolkstein 1978, 30–36)

After the story, I ask them to refer back to their drawing, looking at the box of actuality. I ask,

What things did you hear in the story
that could not have been actual?
Write those outside the box you drew.
What did you hear that was actual?
Write those inside the box.

From there, we can discuss many things: no, owls and roosters do not really date girls nor do they wear clothes or ride horses or go to parties. But the owl *is* nocturnal and has eyes that are sensitive to light. Roosters *can* in a sense be described as elegant and proud, with their colorful appearance and upright heads. In actuality, almost any mother would like at least to see the individual her daughter is going to marry. And as long as we are being actual, certainly some of us have attended parties that lasted until the sun comes up.

Referring back to the idea that we suspend our disbelief (or "see and believe" all that happens while we are in the story circle), students cross over the bridge they drew to the truth of the story. Was there some element of "truth" embedded in it?

Did you recognize something about yourself and
others through the action of the story? By firmly
believing what you heard, no matter how
unbelievable it may have appeared in actuality, do you think
something rang true in the story?

Here we discuss the fact that, yes, people sometimes feel themselves to be ugly, like Owl. We have all felt that. Our self-perceptions often do not correspond to the perceptions others have of us— particularly those who care about us. I ask the children to see these types of "truths" as nuggets—precious knowledge I want them to hold onto—to carry them back to actuality along the path we have drawn.

During a possible follow-up activity, I might suggest this:

As you walk along the path back to the box of
actuality with your "nugget of truth," see if you
can think of one statement or question that relates
that "nugget of truth" to you and people in
general.

Here are the types of statements and questions that have come up:

• The decisions I make can affect the rest of my life.
• People should not jump to conclusions before they know the facts.
• I think friends can be helpful if we just listen to them.
• People are much too critical of themselves.
• Why do we judge ourselves so harshly?
• Why is it sometimes so difficult to trust someone we care for?

Through a series of similar exercises students begin to push the frontiers of their understanding of stories beyond what simply happened. They read seeking meaning. They experience the pleasure of a personal encounter with literature, while finding something worthy of their attention. In the egocentric view of children, the slightest recognition of themselves in the words of another makes a story inherently more valuable. Reading is not simply decoding words in an attempt to comprehend the actions of a story and score well on a test, as some children, alas, come to believe. Instead, reading becomes a self-focused pursuit. We read to see aspects of ourselves in the lives of fictional and nonfictional others. Stories become mirrors to our own nature and actions, thereby putting our experiences into meaningful perspective.

A child's exposure to literature needs to be rich with authentic stories—stories that nurture the child's budding linguistic capabilities and fearlessly curious mind. Stories that are reduced to meager, predetermined sight vocabulary lists or those that have little literary substance or merit run the risk of impoverishing the story experience. As Bettelheim says, "reading becomes devalued when what one reads adds nothing of importance to one's life." The final paragraph of *On Learning to Read,* which he coauthored with Karen Zelan, makes a powerful argument:

The first literature probably consisted of myths, which tried to explain the nature of the world and of man; it was a literature through which man tried to understand himself. Out of myths grew poetry, and later science, the sources of the "two cultures" that are still two avenues for understanding ourselves and the world. If we wish to open the world of literacy to our children, what they are asked to read should from the very beginning help them to understand themselves and their world. Their primers ought to contain only selections that have both meaning and literary merit. From such readers—particularly when we respect how they want to read them—children will be able to learn to read all by themselves, will enjoy it, and will begin their lifelong progress toward ever greater literacy. (Bettelheim and Zelan 1982, 306)

TWO

THE ELEMENTS
OF STORIES

I have come to believe that stories are much like people. From a distance, we are all remarkably similar to each other, but close up, in detail, we are utterly different. From a distance, stories conform to the same shape and display similar features. A story happens in a particular location; it involves a character or characters; their actions or reactions lead to a series of episodes that are somehow brought to resolution by the end of the story. The sequence of a story's events creates a discernible plot in which one episode or event forms the turning point or climax. Much of a story's thrust emanates from an inherent conflict of some kind, and along the way, alert readers may sense a story's theme or central idea. This theme or central idea makes a statement—either directly or implicitly—about life.

Just as most people have the usual complement of arms, fingers, legs, and feet, so most stories have the elements of character, setting, plot, conflict, and central idea. The beauty and uniqueness of a person, however, comes not from what makes that person like every other person but from what makes that person unique. The same is true of stories. The casting and interplay of a story's elements, under the direction of the author's words, determine its uniqueness. The success of a story lies in how well an author (or storyteller) creates a "living person" and how well that person stands out against the background of the story's other elements.

OPENING OR LEAD: A STORY'S FIRST IMPRESSION

In my work with teachers and children, I have found it strange that what I consider to be the most crucial element in a story's initial success is often the most overlooked. A story's first words or lines, or simply how the piece opens, require the very best of the teller. The writer Julia Cunningham, author of *A Mouse Called Junction,* likens the lead sentence of a story to the "opening of a curtain onto the drama to come." If our first impression of a person is often a lasting one, so, too is our first impression of a story. What we first encounter in a story will likely be the factor that determines whether we continue to read or listen to it. In my story performances, I always begin with a catchy story opening, rather than a lengthy discussion about storytelling or a wordy introduction:

Owl thought he was ugly.

The intent, of course, is to catch my listeners' attention. I will have time later for talking or explaining. It is my listeners' desire to know why Owl thought he was ugly and what happens as a consequence that pulls them into the story. The same is true for any written story. Authors want to capture the reader's attention immediately. They will have time and space to ramble later if they

Figure 2–1 "Openings" Signpost

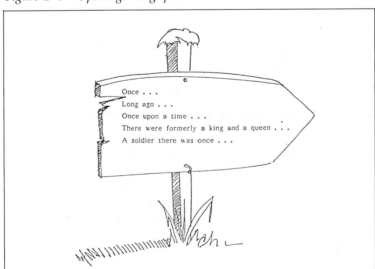

wish. Notice how commanding Evaline Ness's lead is, in her popular children's book, *Sam, Bangs and Moonshine:*

> On a small island, near a large harbor, there once lived a
> fisherman's little daughter (named Samantha, but always called
> Sam), who had the reckless habit of lying. (Ness 1966, 1)

You may notice that I have used the terms *opening* and *lead*
interchangeably. With younger students, I focus on *author's opening,* and with older, more skilled student-writers, I zero in on *lead.*
Let me see if I can illustrate. With primary students, I describe the
author's opening as a signpost that announces the beginning of the
story. A signpost usually indicates the beginning of a hiking trail or
the starting point of a board game like Monopoly. It invites the
reader to experience the story's adventures or to cross over the
bridge (using the "actuality box" metaphor) into the story. In
the classroom, I sometimes write different traditional openings on
large models of signposts (see Figure 2–1).

Openings in printed versions of folk literature function much like
the opening rituals I described in storytelling customs. They beckon
the listener or reader to cross over the bridge and "suspend their
disbelief" or "see and believe all that they hear" and enter the
reality of the story. Similarly, closings in folk literature serve to signal
that the story is over and the reader or listener is to return to the
immediate reality or actuality. I use an ending signpost to illustrate
this (see Figure 2–2).

After telling—or reading—a story in the "story circle," my discussion with young students about openings would go something
like this:

> *Children, did you enjoy the story? Oh, good! It's one of my favor-
> ite stories. Let's see who can remember the author's opening. Won-
> derful. Let's open the book again and find those words. I'll write
> them on our signpost. Now let's read them together. Let's get out
> our other signposts from other stories we've read and notice the
> different ways authors start stories.*

> *What way do you like best? Why? Do you suppose the authors
> thought carefully about starting their stories these different ways?*

The idea of a story opening as an invitation to readers or listeners
can also be used with older students. I suggest to these students
that they try their hand at writing a poetic opening. Figures 2–3 and
2–4 show two examples of my own openings. To bring the listener
into a tale of enchantment, I use the one in Figure 2–3. Or, playing

Figure 2–2 "Closings" Signpost

Figure 2–3 "Enchantment Tale" Signpost

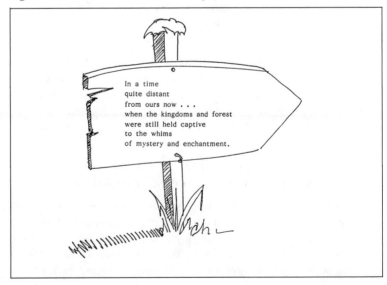

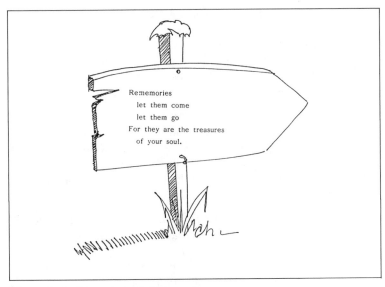

Figure 2–4 "Rememory" Signpost

off the word "rememories" and mimicking the old African opening (see p. 11), I use the one in Figure 2–4 for stories remembered from my own past. In a pile of notes in my study I found an opening one of my students wrote. I like it so much I am using it as the title of this book (see Figure 2–5).

The students in my adult storytelling classes also create openings to use with the stories they tell in their classrooms. Here are several fine examples, which entice listeners to cross over the bridge into the story.

Come with me for a moment in time
  to places deep within your mind,
Where the elephant talks and the flower sings,
You will find wonder in all these things!
                    ROXANNE LOGAN

I believe there's a wondrous place
  suspended somewhere in time and space
Where characters 'live' in the stories we tell
Come—let them weave their magical spell.
                    JOAN BRUNELL

In my writers' workshops with older students, I explain that the lead sentences or paragraph of a story act much like a story opening. They are simply more direct. Donald Murray, author of *Write to Learn,* describes the lead as the "beginning of the beginning" in which the reader decides if he or she is going to read on. Murray says that the entire piece is coiled into the first ten to fifty words. Notice the craft in the opening sentences of *Shadow of a Bull* by Newbery Award winner Maia Wojciechowska:

> When Manolo was nine he became aware of three important facts in his life. First: the older he became, the more he looked like his father. Second: he, Manolo Olivar, was a coward. Third: everyone in the town of Arcangel expected him to grow up to be a famous bullfighter like his father. (Wojciechowska 1964, 3)

In *Experiment with Fiction*, Donald Graves, author of many texts on writing, remarks that "good beginnings bring readers in and help them construct what is to come. . . . A lead is like a promise," he says, a "development of possibility" (Graves 1989, 20). Readers read on to see what will unfold. Here's how one sixth-grade student began a story:

> As Kellen's anxious hands opened her favorite book, *Fantasia,* she was suddenly whisked away into a different land.

Look at her possibilities. Will Kellen become a part of the book she is reading? Why was she so anxious? Has this happened before?

Figure 2–5 Student's Signpost

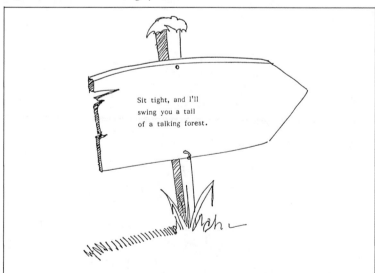

The reader's mind has already constructed both questions and possibilities for the story that will be answered only by reading on.

In my writers' workshops my "author's consideration sheet" (a series of questions for student-authors to consider while rereading the rough drafts of their own stories) contains questions about leads:

- Does my lead grab the reader?
- Have I attempted to entice the reader into continuing on with the story?

The opening or lead in a story attempts to function like the opening notes and phrases of a powerful symphonic piece. To borrow my sixth-grader's wonderful expression, it should "whisk" the listeners away from their cares and responsibilities. Noticing, collecting, and examining openings helps younger children understand how stories are put together. This gives them the beginning of a framework for building their own stories:

Wons upon a tim thr
was a litl boy . . .

Older students, by focusing their attention on lead sentences and paragraphs, move closer to gaining some proficiency with a storywriter's craft. They come to see that the difference between a good lead sentence and an average one is, to use Mark Twain's analogy, the difference between "lightning and the lightning bug."

CHARACTERS: THE SHOULDERS OF A STORY

As all writers of literature for young people know, it is characters that carry the story. If experience has taught them anything about their craft, it is this: no character, no story! Regardless of what else may succeed or fail, the story stands or falls on the "shoulders" of its characters. Walt Morey, author of such fine books as *Gentle Ben* and *Kavik, the Wolf Dog,* has stated that "characterization [in juvenile fiction] has got to be just as good as in an adult book." Even though some characters in the cast are vitally important to the story while others are not, and some are composites of complex traits while others are relatively simple, the strength of a story lies in both the depth and variety of these characters.

As a traveling storyteller, I often return to schools where I have previously appeared. When I ask students what stories they remember from my former visit, never once do they say, "Oh, the story set in the forest," or "The story with the theme of realizing consequences." What they say is, "The story about Bobby and his grandpa" or "The story with the raccoons and the frogs."

Children's literature encompasses an inexhaustible wealth and variety of characters for young readers to meet and come to know. There are delightful characters, devious ones, those with good hearts, those with no hearts at all. There are characters that grow old wisely and others that stay young not so wisely; there are characters from historic times and others who seem like our friends next door. But whatever their natures, or the complexity of their traits, or even the degrees of their importance in a story, characters beckon readers to become more empathetic and understanding of other human beings.

In working with stories and their characters in the classroom, I focus on three areas:

- Understanding a character through a character analysis that emphasizes the physical and behavioral traits of the character.
- Understanding a character through a comparison with another character.
- Understanding the development or changes that a character undergoes in the course of a story.

There are many strategies that can help children understand these elements better. Here are a few I have found useful.

With young children, I have used a *character study sheet* and a "character companion sheet" based in part on the story frames described by Gerald L. Fowler (Fowler 1982). I have used both with an overhead projector, so the whole class could contribute to filling them out, but they can also be used in small reading groups. The character study sheet helps children identify the major character in a story along with his or her actions and their eventual consequences. Figure 2–6 shows an example of the blank sheet. Figure 2–7 shows how a group of second graders used the sheet to respond to Beverly Cleary's *Ramona, Age 8.*

The character companion sheet helps children see that the characters in a story usually look and behave in different ways. It also demonstrates that characters sometimes need to learn a lesson. As the blank sheet in Figure 2–8 shows, children must first record the words they associate with a given character and then explain their choices. "Pierre is stubborn" (from Maurice Sendak's *Pierre*) is acceptable, for example, only if followed with a statement such as "all he will say is 'I don't care.' " It is worth reminding ourselves that characters come to life not through an author's adjectives but through their behavior, actions, and reactions. We come to know characters not so much by how they are described, but by what

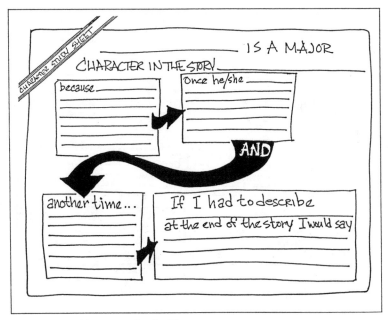

Figure 2–6 Character Study Sheet

Figure 2–7 Completed Character Study Sheet

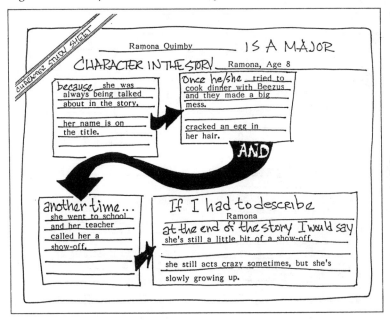

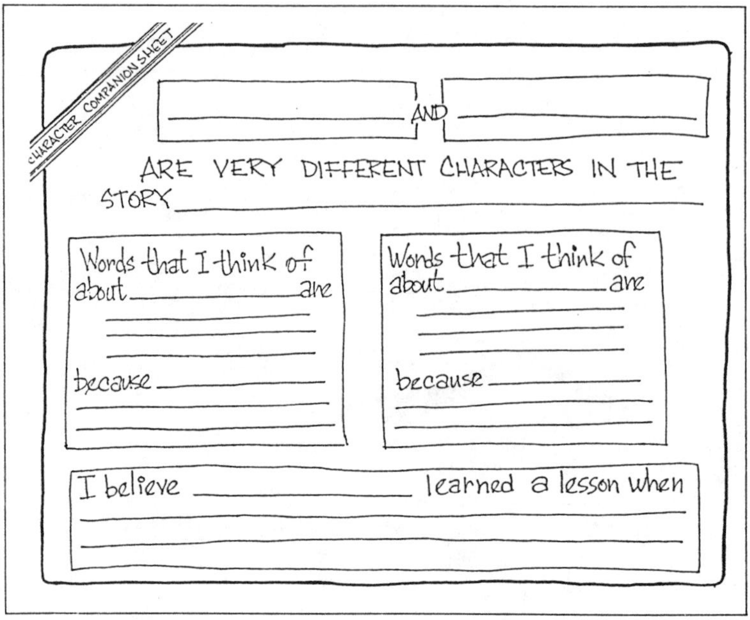

Figure 2–8 Character Companion Sheet

Figure 2–9 Completed Character Companion Sheet

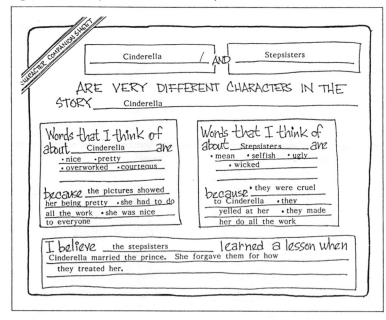

they do as the story unfolds. The children's writer Ouida Sebestyen, author of the highly regarded *Words by Heart,* says that her rule of thumb is not to tell what a character is *like* but to reveal what he *is.* Characters, as a result of their natures or personalities, provoke the action within a story. Having children see this at an early stage encourages them to read with more perception and, in the long run, to write with more power and craft. Figure 2–9 shows a completed character companion sheet for the story of "Cinderella."

Vocabulary enrichment through a *word web* can be used with these sheets as a language arts tie-in. The teacher directs the activity and solicits words and phrases from children to fill out the sheet, and the children see how many synonyms and associated words they can find for each word. Figure 2–10 shows examples of webs for the words *shy,* and *little.*

The class can then decide as a group which word or words from

Figure 2–10 Word Webs

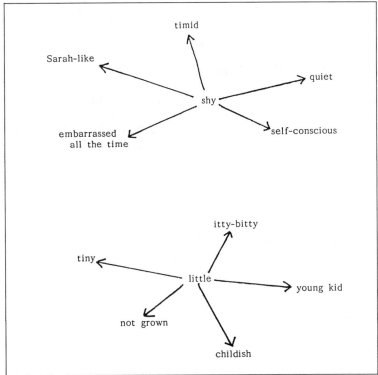

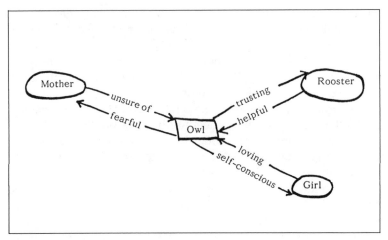

Figure 2–11 Sociogram

the web they want to use on the character sheet and discuss the reasons for their choices. Although some words may mean about the same thing, they come to see that it is the writer's job to find the best word. I often pass along to students an observation Byrd Baylor made in a speech to the International Reading Association: "There are not good or bad words—only more successful words."

The word web can also be used with what Andrea Butler and Jan Turbill have described as a "sociogram" (Butler and Turbill 1987, 54). Students identify the most important person in a story, and we write that person's name in the center of the blackboard. Then we

Figure 2–12 Word Web

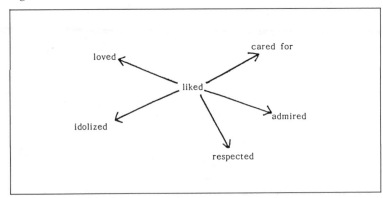

write the names of the other characters in the story around it and draw arrows from each character to the main character and from the main character to each of the others. On each arrow we write a word referring to the feelings of the first character about the one to whom the arrow is pointing. Figure 2–11 shows an example of a sociogram for the story of Owl (see Chapter 1).

I have varied the sociogram described by Butler and Turbill slightly by enclosing the name of the main character in a box and those of the secondary characters in circles to assist the class in distinguishing between them. Like the process involved in the character companion sheet, this exercise may involve creating a word web. If the class says that one character "liked" another, we might brainstorm to find "more successful" words (see Figure 2–12).

In addition to their group applications in the classroom, character sheets, sociograms, and word webs can also be used by more independent students in a listening center. More and more records and cassette tapes of stories told by a variety of storytellers are now available. With a stack of these, some follow-up activity sheets, and a good tape recorder with earphones, an active story listening center can be created in a corner of any classroom.

A final activity for young students is a *character guessing book,* which they can make by folding rectangular sheets of paper and stapling them at the seam. They then fill in the pages with the diagram shown in Figure 2–13.

When the children have made these guessing books for different characters in the story by filling in the appropriate words, they can play a game. One child starts by reading the first page, continuing page by page until someone guesses who the character is. Here is an example:

A CHARACTER POEM

    A

    A *character*

    A *trusting* character

    A *trusting, red-hooded* character

    A *trusting, red-hooded* character *who*
        took a basket of food to her Grandma

    A *trusting, red-hooded* character *who*
        took a basket of food to her Grandma
        in the story *Little Red Riding Hood*

As students become more mature as readers and the characters they encounter in their reading become more complex, the type of

PAGE NUMBER	TEXT
1	A
2	A CHARACTER
3	A ___(1)___ CHARACTER
4	A ___(1)___ , ___(2)___ CHARACTER
5	A ___(1)___ , ___(2)___ CHARACTER WHO ___(3)___
6	A ___(1)___ , ___(2)___ CHARACTER WHO ___(3)___ IN THE STORY ___(4)___
7	A ___(1)___ , ___(2)___ CHARACTER WHO ___(3)___ IN THE STORY ___(4)___ BY ___(5)___

Key to numbers in parentheses:
(1) = behavior trait
(2) = physical trait
(3) = illustrating incident
(4) = title of story
(5) = author of story

Figure 2–13 Character Guessing Book

character analysis they do can be expanded. I want students to come to know their characters as well as a professional actor knows the character he or she is portraying on stage or in film. It may be of interest to students that some writers make extensive notes about a fictional character—everything from the character's favorite food to his or her shoe size—long before using him or her in a story. It is through such attention to detail that writers are able to create characters that seem real.

Borrowing an idea from another children's writer, J. P. Petersen, author of *How Can You Hijack a Cave?,* I've used an exercise that involves his three-sentence character sketches. Over the years I have gathered a collection of interesting magazine photographs of faces— old faces, innocent young faces, sad faces, smiling faces—from a whole array of cultures and backgrounds. I spread these pictures out in the classroom and each student picks one that particularly appeals to him or her. The students spend some time thinking about the person behind the face and then write a three-sentence character sketch that includes the following:

- One sentence about the person's past history.
- One sentence of physical description.
- One imagined direct quotation from the person.

I have them consider as much as they can about the person:

- name
- age
- personality (what's inside)
- daily appearance (what's outside)
- relationships
- occupation
- hobbies
- health
- economic status
- goals

"Dig inside," I say.

- Where is she from?
- Does he like his job?
- Where does he shop?
- What was (is) her relationship with her parents?
- What is the last book he read?
- Does she attend church?
- What are his favorite foods?
- What are her worst fears?
- What are his dreams?
- Etc.

This exercise forces students to develop a mental picture of a character even before they have devised a plot. Often, students create characters solely to fill in the action in their plot, which more than likely leaves their characters flat, underdeveloped, and cartoonlike. If students eventually use the faces from this exercise in a story (as most do), they must remain true to their original sketches.

In studying characters from other stories, I've had students use a *character ladder* (see Figure 2–14) to begin their character analysis. The character ladder functions much like the character companion

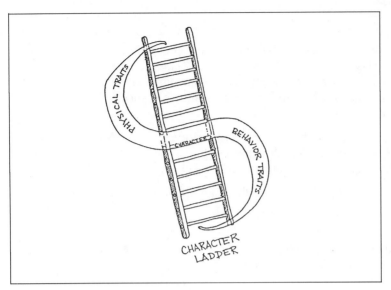

Figure 2–14 Character Ladder

Figure 2–15 Because Box

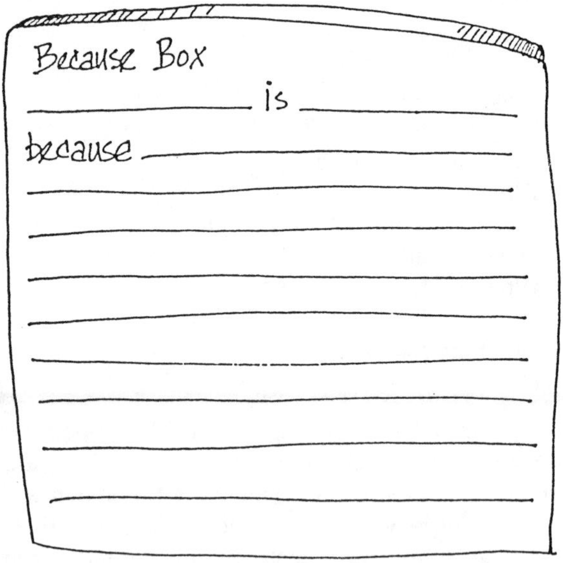

sheet (see Figure 2–8) I use with younger students. I ask students to find words that describe the physical and behavioral traits of a character. I explain that physical traits are on the "outside" of the person—we can easily see them—while behavior traits are often on the "inside" of the character. We need to watch and listen to characters to see these traits. "Behavior traits," I explain to my students, "are revealed by the character much more than they are told by the author." Beyond simply saying that a character is mean or unhappy, students must justify their description by filling in a "because box" (see Figure 2–15) to demonstrate how the character is revealed.

The because box forces students to discover what is actually "given" in the story. They must look harder and dig deeper for what the author says *or* implies. They must identify the information the author means to give away in the text. The following sentence starters can help students complete the because box:

- Because we are shown on page . . .
- Because the author clearly states that . . .
- Because the character says . . .
- Because the character did . . .
- Because the character thinks . . .
- Because the character demonstrates . . .
- Because the other characters say about him/her . . .
- Because the other characters react to him/her in this way . . .
- Because the other characters say to him/her . . .

Figure 2–16 shows an example of a character ladder for Miss Moody in Brinton Turkle's *Do Not Open,* while Figure 2–17 shows how a fifth grader responded to Scrooge in Charles Dickens's *A Christmas Carol.*

Another approach to encourage older students in more in-depth character analysis is to have them role-play as detectives. The scenario might go something like this. The class is reading Beverly Cleary's *Ramona the Brave.* Students are given the following assignment to complete as they read:

DETECTIVE ASSIGNMENT
given to _____

Case: A little girl named Ramona Quimby, from the pages of Beverly Cleary's book, *Ramona the Brave,* is missing. Her parents, Mr. and Mrs. Quimby, reported that she disappeared on May 28 and has not been seen or heard from since. In order to solve the mystery, you must first find out as much about Ramona as possible. You will need to know her inside and out from the clues the author gives in the

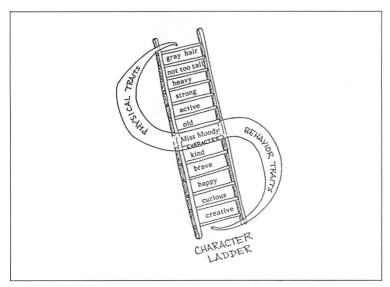

Figure 2–16 Completed Character Ladder

book. Everything you find in the book will be solid evidence about her character. You will therefore need to report the page number or numbers on which you find the evidence. Here is what you are to look for:
- What does she look like?
- How does she normally act?
- Does she speak in a distinctive manner?
- What can you determine about how she thinks? How she feels?
- How do you think she appears to others? Name the others.
- What have the other characters said about her?

Another valuable strategy for looking at characters is to have students evaluate an author's characterization. Reading classes may be divided into small groups and each group given a different character from a story or a short novel. Each group then fills out a *characterization evaluation sheet* (see Figure 2–18) by discussing and scoring the author's success with characterization.

This type of analysis can also be the basis for a "group critique"

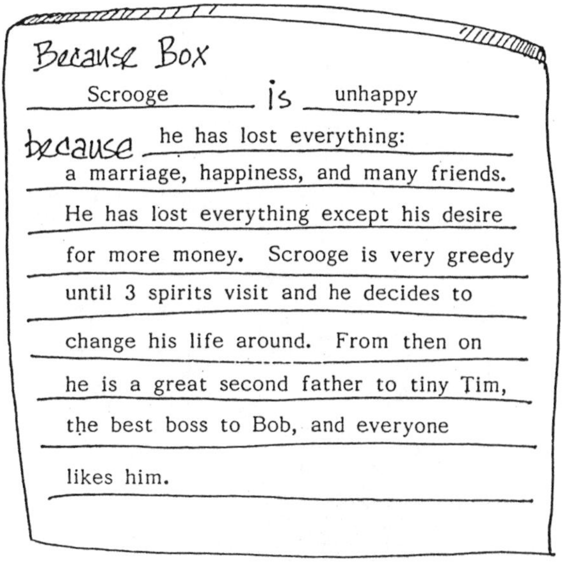

Figure 2–17 Completed Because Box

or "self-evaluation" of students' own stories. They can use the same newly trained, critical eye they have used in evaluating characters in stories and books in looking at their own efforts. Through directed activities and discussions such as these, older students can be encouraged to read with a "deeper eye" and to discover how authors give form and substance to their characters. They can begin to work with the basic tools of literary criticism, and, finally, to challenge their own writing skills through the characters they create in their stories.

Above all, I want my students to see that characters are not stone sculptures, cast in one posture forever, but like all of us, are constantly changing. Betsy Byars, Newbery Award winner for her book *Summer of the Swans*, stated in a speech that the thread most common to all protagonists in modern children's fiction is that they change somewhere in the course of the story. It is surely true that if characters did not forgive, summon hidden courage, mature, learn acceptance, and eventually achieve deeper understanding, these characters, and indeed, their stories, would be of less value and interest.

Often the quiet, yet significant changes a character undergoes

Characterization Evaluation Sheet

Character's name _____

from _____

by _____

A character is revealed by how he or she looks, acts, thinks, and feels.
How well did the author do?

Physical description

1	2	3	4	5	6	7	8	9	10

| Boo, never once did this author attempt to paint a picture of the character! | | | Coming into visual focus, but a bit vague – still need more descriptive information. | | | Now there's a character that can be seen vividly. This author chose each description carefully. | | | |

Actions

1	2	3	4	5	6	7	8	9	10

| Dry! Dead on the page! Character dies here! Call the morgue! | | | Up and walking, but the author still needs to *show* the reader who the character is through his/her behavior. | | | Excellent! This character lives! The reader learned more about the character with every page. | | | |

Thoughts and Feelings

1	2	3	4	5	6	7	8	9	10

| This character's a zombie – no feelings. Didn't the author want the reader to get inside the character? | | | Better... but even a psychologist would have a hard time knowing what makes this character tick. | | | This character is a real person; reading this was like coming to know, really know, a new friend. | | | |

Overall Analysis

1	2	3	4	5	6	7	8	9	10

| Junk! Reader never got to know this character. Back to the drawing board. | | | Halfway there – good work, but still could be developed more. | | | Top honors! Here is a character that will live in the minds of the readers. | | | |

Figure 2–18 Character Evaluation Sheet

are best identified and brought out in an open-ended readers' re-action or discussion group. Students may be able to see changes best through the use of a story time line. While reading Wilson Rawls's wonderful novel, *The Summer of the Monkeys,* for example, my third graders each began to map out a time line of the actions of the book's main character, Jay Berry. They illustrated these ep-isodes on a long, narrow strip of butcher paper. When the time line was completed, we talked about how Jay Berry felt and behaved at different points in the story.

- How did Jay Berry feel after this incident?
- What do you think was most important to him here? Why?
- How did he feel toward his parents? His sister? His grandpa?
- Were you surprised when he did that? Why do you think he did? What would you have done, given the same situation?
- How do you think Jay Berry is viewed by his parents, sister, and grandpa here?

By examining a character's behavior and reactions over time, students have the opportunity to appreciate the changes that people naturally go through. People rarely change overnight. The same is true of a story character. Being able to notice how characters change makes the reading more rewarding to the reader and affords an ideal chance for them to become aware of the changes they themselves will go through in the course of their own lives.

SETTING: A STORY'S STAGE

If characters and their actions carry the weight of a story, the setting surrounds it with a frame, giving it specific boundaries in time and space or creating a particular atmosphere. The setting functions as a verbal backdrop for the story in the reader's or listener's mind.

Settings in stories for young people vary widely. They may include elaborate details that describe every delicious detail—sight, smell, and sound—as in Willy Wonka's chocolate factory in Roald Dahl's *Charlie and the Chocolate Factory.* Or they may be only "bare bones" sets, as in a folktale that says no more than "Once long ago in a deep forest in a humble hut. . . . " All writers must carefully consider how much description a story's setting needs. In one story, specific details may be necessary to the plot or overall purpose, while in another, the writer may only want to include a well-selected image or two and allow readers to imagine the rest for themselves.

In my work, I have learned that children will not sit still for drawn-out descriptions of a setting (or anything else, for that matter—with the exception of food or Halloween gore). Nor do they have a natural tendency to describe the setting in the stories they write. As adults we can sit back and bask in the lush details on page after page as Marjorie Rawlings describes the land and foliage of central Florida in her book *Cross Creek*. Children, with their hyperkinetic reading style, will not tolerate it. They insist on getting to the action, and the sooner the better. Writers who are sensitive to this fact include only enough description to create the effect they want without taxing the patience of their young readers.

Whether the author is elaborate or restrained in the use of details, the setting is very much a part of a story's design. In *The Ghost Eye Tree,* Bill Martin Jr and John Archambault begin to create an eerie mood with lines such as these:

> *One dark and windy autumn night when the sun*
> *had long gone down . . .*

> *Why does Mama always choose me when the night*
> *is so dark and the mind runs free?*

Setting may function in a story as an antagonist. In Jean Craighead George's *Julie of the Wolves* or Gary Paulsen's *Dogsong,* the cold, unforgiving Arctic climate propels the story. Settings may also reflect a historical context. Cynthia Rylant's *When I Was Young in the Mountains* nostalgically recreates an Appalachian mountain community, and there are many other similar examples of historical fiction written for young people.

In the broad field of children's literature, however, an author's text is not the only source of information about the setting. Illustrated books and picture books also allow the reader to experience the story through the illustrator's interpretation. The visual elements (color, line, shape, and texture) and the artistic media used by the illustrator can contribute another dimension to the reader's sense of a story's setting. Delicate lines and soft watercolor washes, for example, can convey the impression of a magical or enchanted place as clearly as any words. Having young children examine and discuss the pictures in their illustrated books will help them see how the text and visual arts blend together to tell the story.

When I tell traditional tales, it is as if children have a rough pen-and-ink sketch of a classic setting already in their minds; my words merely fill it in. I do not have to describe a castle or a kingdom for my audiences to understand where a story involving the activities of kings and queens, princesses and princes takes place. Words such as "a certain kingdom," "deep woods," "simple hut," "warm and pleasant land," and "magical kingdom" are all they need to envision the setting. What the author or teller describes, how the illustrator does his job, and what mental pictures the child already has all work together.

In the classroom, I have used *setting sheets* with primary-grade students (see Figure 2–19) because I have found that they elicit a more perceptive understanding of a story's setting. Like the character sheets, these could be used in whole class discussion, with a small reading group in a collaborative effort, or as an independent activity sheet in a reading center. See Figure 2–20 for some examples of students' work using the sheet with the picture book *The Little Red Hen* by Paul Galdone.

In the writing center in my classroom I used to keep small plastic bags labeled with the names of different places in which a story could take place: desert, forest, tropical island, castle, city, park, and so on. Each bag held a collection of small strips of paper on

Figure 2–19 Setting Sheet

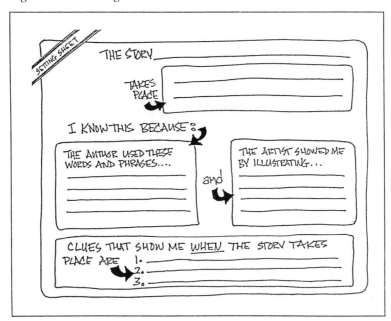

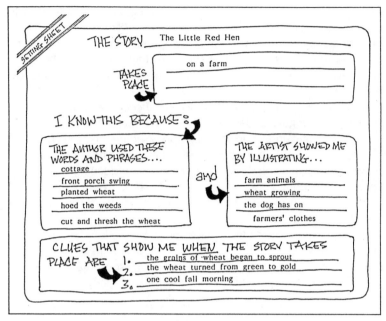

THE STORY ___The Little Red Hen___

TAKES PLACE — on a farm

I KNOW THIS BECAUSE:

THE AUTHOR USED THESE WORDS AND PHRASES....
cottage
front porch swing
planted wheat
hoed the weeds
cut and thresh the wheat

and

THE ARTIST SHOWED ME BY ILLUSTRATING...
farm animals
wheat growing
the dog has on
farmers' clothes

CLUES THAT SHOW ME WHEN THE STORY TAKES PLACE ARE
1. the grains of wheat began to sprout
2. the wheat turned from green to gold
3. one cool fall morning

Figure 2–20 Completed Setting Sheet

which were written types of characters, objects, plants, and other items typical of that particular setting. In the *desert* bag, for instance, were:

lizard
yucca plant
iguana
cactus
sand
rocks
eagles
rodents
snakes
coyotes
clouds
sun's heat

If a child wanted to place a story in one of these settings, the bag provided a ready-made, brainstormed word list. Throughout the year we would gather "setting words" from many diverse places as students came back from vacations or travels wanting to make their own *Hawaii bag* or *ski area bag.*

Using the word list as a jumping-off place, we could experiment by putting characters in unusual settings. The idea of an Eskimo in the desert or a hermit in a shopping mall sets up a situation ripe for the imagination. Many children's writers have employed this same technique. We have Sendak's dog in a vaudeville act in *Higglety, Pigglety, Pop,* a pack of mice as shipmates aboard a clipper in Steven Kellogg's *The Island of the Skog,* an elephant sitting on a bird's nest in Dr. Seuss's *Horton Hatches the Egg,* or a cantankerous donkey who smokes in Ellen Raskin's *Moe Q McGlutch, He Smoked Too Much;* and the list could go on.

To help children experiment independently, I created a *writer's flip book* for my classroom writing center. It had eleven different characters, eleven descriptive adjectives for those characters, and eleven choices of settings. Here are the lists:

CHOOSE ONE FROM EACH LIST:

List 1	*List 2*	*List 3*
weary	hermit	cottage
gentle	farmer	cave
bored	scoundrel	igloo
lonesome	priest	city
monstrous	merchant	village
angry	hunter	castle
shy	king	jungle
merry	princess	sea
stingy	spider	ghetto
mean	robber	forest
friendly	knight	desert

By flipping through the book, individual students could discover a large number of possible story combinations:

- friendly robber in a ghetto
- stingy princess in a cave
- gentle hunter in a jungle

To help them get started, I gave them these story questions to consider:

- Why is the character in the situation he/she is in?
- What is the cause of the predicament?
- Does he/she want to change the situation?
- What will he/she do?
- Are there any difficulties encountered by his/her actions?
- What are the consequences of his/her actions?
- Will he/she ever resolve the problem?
- What could happen as a result of the resolution?
- What can bring the story to an end?

In working with older students, I want them to see that a precise description of the setting, when carefully interwoven into a tale, offers an element of realism. Whether stories are realistic fiction or pure invention and fantasy, they should create the illusion of reality. William Sleator, author of some very fine science fiction for young adults, contends that creating a credible setting in fantasy is much more difficult than in realistic fiction since in the former he has to convince his readers before they buy into the story line that his setting *could* exist. "In realistic fiction they already know that the reality exists." The test of any writer is in his ability to convince our reading minds of the reality of his story, whatever its actual authenticity. Stories set in the Appalachian Mountains need to ring true; the texture and flavor of the mountain setting must be successfully conveyed. A story centered around city life must be imbued with an urban reality. Even the wildest fantasy must be set *somewhere,* and the writer has to make that somewhere believable.

One of the illustrations I have used with my students in writers' workshops plays off the metaphor of the setting as the "story's stage." I would draw a line on the blackboard with *Bona Fide Broadway* on one end and *Bare Bones* on the other:

BONA FIDE	BARE
BROADWAY	BONES

I would talk about how the setting is the stage on which the story's characters perform. I would ask them to imagine or recall an elaborate Broadway musical production, with its lavish costumes and intricate sets (perhaps the recent production of *Cats* would be a good example). That is a "bona fide Broadway" setting. I then read several of the more detailed passages from Kenneth Grahame's *The*

Wind in the Willows to illustrate the same thing in prose. Next I suggested that they visualize a simple set with only a couple of boxes for props and a drop cloth with a few painted trees for a background and read them part of a folktale particularly sparse in detail. The simple stage was its appropriate, "bare bones" setting. I want to communicate the idea that neither setting is necessarily better. Each serves the design of its story. When they write their own stories, their settings will probably lie somewhere between the "bona fide Broadway" and the "bare bones." "You, as authors," I would tell them,

> *need to act like theater producers and decide what details and de-scriptions you want to put in each set or episode. You need to think about exactly what you want the readers to 'see' in their heads in each part of your story.*

Much of the success of any literary setting is the result of the clarity of its descriptions. Clarity is achieved through the use of concrete details—details that appeal to the readers' senses. Notice the details Grahame incorporates into this paragraph from *The Wind in the Willows* in which Mole goes out to explore the Wild Wood.

> It was a cold still afternoon with a hard steely sky overhead, when he slipped out of the warm parlour into the open air. The country lay bare and entirely leafless around him, and he thought that he had never seen so far and so intimately into the insides of things as on that winter day when Nature was deep in her annual slumber and seemed to have kicked the clothes off. Copses, dells, quarries and all hidden places, which had been mysterious mines for exploration in leafy summer, now exposed themselves and their secrets pathetically, and seemed to ask him to overlook their shabby poverty for a while, till they could riot in rich masquerade as before, and trick and entice him with the old deceptions. It was pitiful in a way, and yet cheering—even exhilarating. He was glad that he liked the country undecorated, hard, and stripped of its finery. He had got down to the bare bones of it, and they were fine and strong and simple. He did not want the warm clover and the play of seeding grasses; the screens of quickset, the billowy drapery of beech and elm seemed best away; and with great cheerfulness of spirit he pushed on towards the Wild Wood, which lay before him low and threatening, like a black reef in some still southern sea.

Having older students examine this passage and others like it, helps them discover how rich, sensory pictures can be created with well-crafted words and phrases. As a class project my students and I would select Grahame's best sensory images:

cold still afternoon
hard steely sky overhead
lay bare and entirely leafless
he thought that he had never seen so far and so intimately into
    the insides of things
deep in her annual slumber
seemed to have kicked the clothes off
exposed themselves and their secrets pathetically
shabby poverty
riot in rich masquerade
stripped of its finery
play of seeding grasses
billowy drapery of beech and elm
great cheerfulness of spirit

Phrases such as these would, I hoped, become the benchmark for what students attempted in their own writing. So that they would become more aware of sensory words and phrases, we would from time to time keep a checklist of words from their own writing that appealed to their sense of smell, sight, taste, hearing, and physical touch.

A final note. I discovered that my comments to students about their use of description in their stories (or the lack of it) worked best when I focused on exactly what they as writers wanted the reader to see and how they accomplished that task in their text. This has proved far more effective than simply encouraging them to add description for its own sake. Too many details can destroy a story as readily as too few. Ouida Sebestyen suggests that writers not interrupt the plot to describe a setting, but sneak in details as they move the story along. In a later section, I will offer further strategies for using setting in different story genres.

PROBLEM OR CONFLICT: A STORY'S DRIVING FORCE

Imagine, if you will, a perfect world—a world where people are happy, content, well-fed, clothed, warm, where there is no discontentment, no envy, no greed, no yearning, no sadness. Utter bliss! you might think. Now ask yourself, would there be stories in such a world?

I suspect not.

Stories arise from the problems and conflicts of our lives, from our own imperfections and the imperfections of the world around us. Tolstoy's *War and Peace* does not portray an Eden-like world, whose inhabitants are happy and contented, but a world in turmoil. The driving force of any story—be it children's literature or adult fiction—is the inherent conflicts and problems experienced by its characters.

Returning to my writer's flip book, what if I had included only two lists, character and setting? Would there be a story? For example:

farmer in a field
> or
eagle in the mountains

There isn't much of a story in either of these without some sort of conflict or problem. But if I add "lonely" to the "farmer in a field," then I have the makings of a story. Why is he lonely? Where is his family? What has happened to his friends? What will he do to relieve his loneliness? What will be the consequences of those actions? And if I add "wounded" to the "eagle in the mountains," I have the beginnings of an animal survival story. All stories come to life through conflict—whether caused by greed, need, the complications of life in society, misunderstandings, determination against odds, human survival, helplessness, desire. In a talk before the National Council of Teachers of English in 1988 the actress and writer Maya Angelou suggested that all literature is at its root a code to surviving in the world . . . and doing so with some class and compassion.

The conflict in a story is best discussed in terms of the motivation of its central characters: motivation causes or provokes a character's behavior, which then further illuminates the character's motivation—to gain riches without effort, for example, or to be accepted by others at any cost. But the motivation might also be the desire to provide for a family or to achieve a happier life. All stories are versions of three basic types of conflict:

- Conflict with nature.
- Conflict with other people (and/or society).
- Conflict with self.

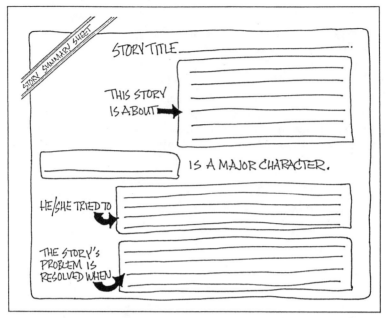

Figure 2–21 Story Summary Sheet

Figure 2–22 Completed Story Summary Sheet

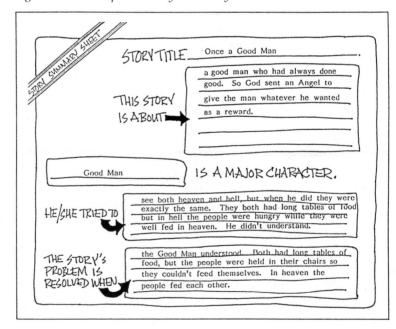

If you examine any of the stories you read or assign to your class, you will probably find one or more of these conflicts played out through its characters.

When children identify the basic problem or conflict in a story, they take the first step in their development as perceptive readers. This type of perception doesn't come overnight, like a light bulb flashing on, but slowly through exposure to a wide variety of stories under the nurturing guidance of a literate teacher. Consideration of a story's main problem or conflict should be part of any group discussion of a story.

• Who can tell me the problem in this story?
• When did you first discover or get hints about the problem?
• How did the author show us the problem?
• Who can tell me what might have motivated the character to behave as he or she did?
• Have you ever experienced the same desires?
• Does this conflict remind you of any other stories?

With younger students, I have used a *story summary sheet* (see Figure 2–21) to help them organize a story around its problem and that problem's eventual resolution. Figure 2–22 shows one completed by a group of second graders for the story "Once a Good Man" by Jane Yolen from the book *The Hundredth Dove and Other Tales.*

Another sheet that allows students to focus on a story's problem and do a quick analysis is a *story statement sheet.* There were copies of the story summary sheet in the reading center in my classroom to be used as independent activities when students had a few moments of free time. They could choose to pick up a book (which was likely to be from a collection of short picture books) and fill out the sheet to keep in their reading folders. Figure 2–23 shows a sample done on Mercer Mayer's delightful book *Just for You.*

Periodically during the school year, I would have students pull out their reading folders for review, and we would categorize the books and stories we had read by the type of conflict they exemplified. I would draw a huge pie, each section labeled with a type of conflict, on the board, and we would fill it in (see Figure 2–24). We often discussed how some books and stories shared two, or possibly all three, types of conflicts.

In a similar way, I would ask older students to map out the stories they were writing themselves. They used the author's questions from story sequence sheets to help them focus and shape their stories (see Figure 2–25).

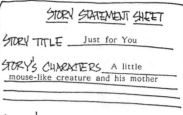

Figure 2–23
Completed Story
Statement Sheet

STORY STATEMENT SHEET

STORY TITLE ____Just for You____

STORY'S CHARACTERS ___A little___
__mouse-like creature and his mother__
_____

STORY'S SETTING __In their home__
_____
_____

STORY'S PROBLEM ___The little___
__mouse-like creature wants to help his__
__mother, but only makes a bigger__
__mess when he does.__

STORY'S RESOLUTION __The little___
__mouse-like creature finally does__
__something special for his mom--__
__he kisses her!__
_____

NAME _____

Figure 2–24 Conflict Pie

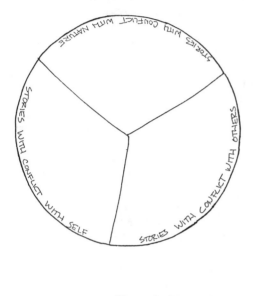

Figure 2–25 Author's Questions

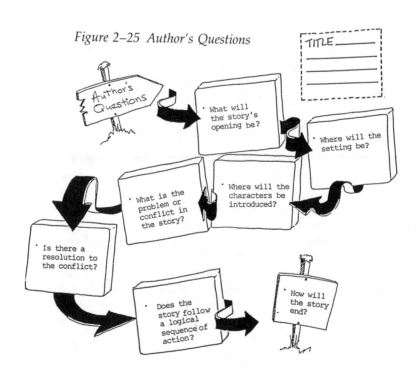

A conflict is crucial to the makings of a story, but if the conflict has no resolution it is like a ball tossed high in the air that does not return to earth. The story seems to lack optimism or hope. When a story grows out of the imperfections of life, the crises (major or minor) of humans—or animals acting like humans—as they live out their lives, the resolution of these problems is the story's saving grace. It establishes in the reader's mind a sense of order and fairness about the world.

PLOT AND RESOLUTION: THE DESIGN OF A STORY'S ACTION

Young writers too often employ two techniques to resolve their stories. You may recognize them. One I call the *pencil lift-off*. The other is in the ever-popular *it-was-only-a-dream* tradition.

In the pencil lift-off ending, the writer ends his or her story by coming to a point and simply launching the pencil straight into the air. This is accompanied by the familiar termination statement, "I'm done!" What this technique essentially demonstrates, however, is that the student has run out of ideas, or energy, or both. If we look closely at the story just completed, it more than likely represents a string of action events, one after another, that comes to an abrupt end. What this illustrates is that the student lacked an organizational design to guide the story. No beginning, no middle, no end; no rising action with some sort of turning point; no conclusion; no planned progression toward the resolution of a demonstrated problem. Just one action event after another. Anyone who has taught writing has read far too many examples of stories like these.

In the second type of ending, the child will resolve everything in the story with these words: "But it was only a dream, and I woke up." Again, the student's work is marred not necessarily by a lack of desire or effort but by the absence of a structure or organizational design. It is probably characterized by a series of poorly developed, cartoonlike (often violent) episodes that simply run out of steam (or everyone in the story is killed off). The only way out is to declare that it was "only a dream."

Helping beginning writers to overcome these tendencies may be accomplished in part by showing them that stories have a shape. Unlike the series of actions performed by a person in the course of a day (get out of bed, rub eyes, shower, eat breakfast, get dressed for school), a story is a structured sequence of events chosen by the author to reveal an aspect of a character or of the story's situation. Ouida Sebestyen expresses the author's point of view when she says, "If fully realized characters have a really hard problem, they create their own action." Such actions are not random occurrences in the life of the character, but selected moments the author has consciously decided to highlight. They revolve around the basic story line and move toward a resolution of some kind. This constitutes the story's plot.

A well-designed plot goes somewhere. As we follow the story's action, we come to know the characters and to understand the motivation behind their actions. We may feel empathy for them, or we may look forward to seeing them get their just reward. Along the way, we can predict the possible turn of events, and we wait to see what happens.

Children need to know that authors have the option (and the duty) to rearrange, alter, or delete events in order to further their plot and maintain a degree of tension within their story. They are under no obligation to any strictly chronological sequence of events. In fact, they are free to ignore details if those details do not seem necessary to the story. The prolific children's writer Clyde Robert Bulla states it his way:

> What can I say about plot? You know about the beginning, middle and end. You introduce an interesting character and give him or her a problem. Let him or her try to solve the problem. In the end let him or her either solve the problem or be overcome by it. You create action by bringing opposing forces together.

A classroom teacher can offer guided instruction to help students understand story design in three general ways: by examining the design principles behind stories, by modeling the story composition process, and by using story planning strategies.

Examining design principles

With primary students I often use a *story plot sheet* (see Figure 2–26) to help them see how simple stories are designed and held together. This sheet gives them experience in recognizing the story's problem, the order of its episodes, and its resolution. Figure 2–27 records a class collaboration about the traditional story, "The Three Billy Goats Gruff."

The story sheet also shows students how authors use sequence *clue words*—such as *after that, next,* or *finally*—to help them or-

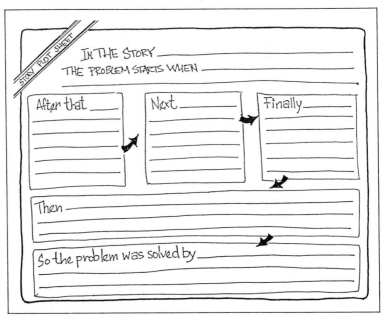

Figure 2–26 Story Plot Sheet

Figure 2–27 Completed Story Plot Sheet

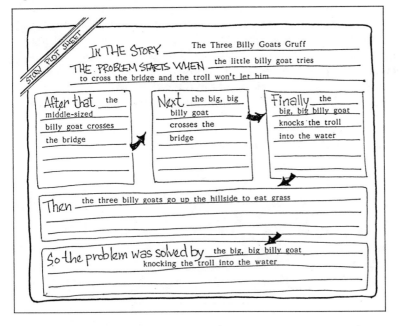

ganize the action in the story. They kept a list of other clue words in their writing folders.

> The next morning . . .
> Finally . . .
> Next . . .
> It wasn't long before . . .
> At the start . . .
> First . . .
> After that . . .
> To begin with . . .
> At the end . . .
> Last . . .
> Then . . .

Another design model is the *rising and falling action triangle* (see Figure 2–28). Although there are many different story patterns, and variations on each, this popular diagram helps children visualize the shape of a story. A more elaborate model, which I referred to as a "Story Plot Path" and used with students, appears in Figure 2–29. As the Story Plot Path demonstrates, many stories conform to a basic design. After we had heard or read a story, we followed the model together on the overhead screen, identifying the story's opening and discussing the characters and the setting. As the story moved along the "plot path," we tried to determine its basic problem and identify the succeeding episodes and events along the way. At the highest point (the flag), we talked about how the conflict or problem was at last resolved and how all the loose ends were tied up. Finally, we saw how the story's closing fit into the design.

Figure 2–30 shows how the Story Plot Path model works with an

Figure 2–28 Rising and Falling Action Triangle

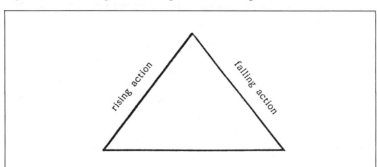

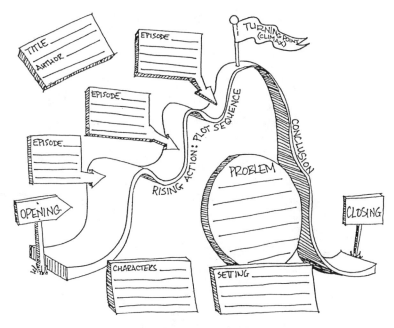

Figure 2–29 Story Plot Path

Figure 2–30 Filled-in Story Plot Path

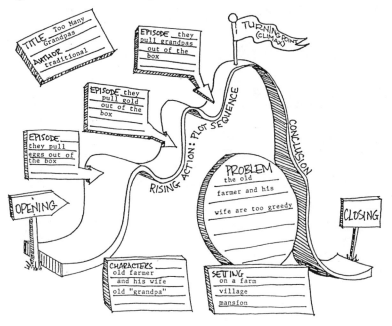

old folktale, "Too Many Grandpas." Here is a summary of the story.

> An old farmer and his wife are very poor. One day, while
> working in the field, the farmer finds an old box. When he
> brings it home, his wife accidentally drops an egg into it. From
> then on, each time they pull an egg out of the box, another is
> found in its place. They sell all of these eggs for a few pieces
> of gold. They find that when they drop a piece of gold into the
> box and then take it out, another piece of gold appears. Soon
> they are very rich; but they also become quite greedy and
> apparently rather lazy. They decide they would prefer not to
> have to gather the gold from the box themselves, so they ask
> their grandpa to do it for them. The grandpa eventually falls
> into the box. The couple has to spend all of their money
> burying grandpa after grandpa as they pull them out of the
> box. They end up just as poor as they started.

The tale includes these story elements:

Opening	Once there was an old farmer and his wife who were so poor, all they had were . . .
Climax	So they had to spend all their money burying all the grandpas they pulled out of the box.
Conclusion	They took the box with the grandpa in it back out to that farm. They dug a hole and put the box back in the ground.
Closing	And after being so greedy, they ended up just as poor as before. And that's the story of too many grandpas.

In the primary classroom, a story summary model can be constructed on the floor with masking tape. Children then literally
"walk" through the shape of the story, retelling parts of it as they
go along. I've also experimented with hand-held road signs in-
scribed with the opening and closing words and sequence clue
words, which individual students hold up while they walk along
the model:

• Once there lived an . . .
• One day . . .
• The next day . . .
• Finally . . .
• And after being so greedy . . .

Intermediate students can use this model as a prewriting guide to composing a traditional story. They can also use it at home to analyze the plots of their favorite television shows.

Although I hardly need say so, many favorite stories do not fit comfortably into either the story summary sheet or rising action model. These are probably not the best examples to use in looking at story design. Many others do, and many of the folktales so popular with young children certainly do. As simple as this three-episode, rising-falling model may appear, it is the foundation of much fiction writing. Pat Rhoads Mauser, a wonderful writer of juvenile fiction, explained to a group of my students that when she begins an outline for one of her books, she develops the idea for her characters first and then determines the first and last pages of the book. But she doesn't start writing until she has identified three "complications" for her characters. The "magic three" (as the model has been called) is a structure young readers will encounter frequently throughout their reading lives.

Teacher modeling of the composition process

Every day children see adults doing many things, but rarely, if ever, do they see adults engaged in the composition process. In *Joining the Literacy Club* Frank Smith notes:

> Many teachers are surprised when they reflect upon what they actually demonstrate to children about reading and writing during the school day. How many teachers are seen reading a novel or a magazine for pleasure? What might children assume reading and writing to be from the kinds of written language activity they see teachers engaging in? (Smith 1988, 12)

In my own home, my stepdaughter sees me at my desk, pencil in hand, notes and books everywhere. Later, she may see the re-sult—a poem or a story or an article. What she has seen, however, is not the composition process, but external behavior, the kind of activities writers in movies engage in—sitting at desks, not saying a word. What my stepdaughter does not see is how I shift around and organize ideas in my head, make lists, check references, jot down a phrase, cross out a word, choose one expression over another, stare at the page as I wonder what to tell the reader. She is not aware of the hundreds of silent questions I ask myself as I work on a piece. These are the kinds of mental processes that go on in a writer's head, and these are the processes that children need to know about and engage in themselves if they are to become skilled writers.

In my classroom, I would often have children collaborate with me in the story-writing process using an overhead projector. Although each session was spontaneous and unique, several common threads characterized all of them. They all included

- A review of story terminology—character, setting, plot, conflict, motivation, climax, resolution, opening, closing, and so on. The children came to use these terms with increasing ease and authority. "Let's have our main character make one big mistake," says Mike. "Let's create a real suspenseful climax and try to catch our reader off guard," says Cheryl.
- *A restatement of author questions*—how real writers go about "conferencing" with themselves while shaping a story out of a story idea. "Who can tell me what we should be thinking about with our lead sentences?" I ask. "What other ways might we get that idea across?" "Will we confuse the reader with this?" "Surely we can find a better description here." "What do we really want the reader to be seeing now?"
- *Practice and rehearsal of the writing process*—student participation in making decisions about everything that goes into a story: characters' names and how their motivations are to be revealed, as well as setting, and dialogue, mood and action.

Through repeated exposure to collaborative story-writing sessions, using the same terms over and over, rehearsing the same author questions and concerns again and again, and participating in the composition process (however varied the final outcome), children soon internalized these activities and began including them when they wrote independently. In the process of repeatedly using these strategies, they started to observe how, in the creation of a story, character, conflict, setting, and plot are all co-conspirators.

Story-planning strategies

The element critical to determining the success of a child's story has little to do with skill in spelling, punctuation, sentence structure, or grammar. It has little to do with persistence—getting around to finishing the piece—and even less to do with reading ability (except, of course, in severely deficient students). The most crucial difference between the best of my story writers and the worst can be measured by the hands of my watch: *time.* By this I mean that what is most important is the length of time from the story idea to the first sentence. This is not to imply that the skills of spelling, punctuation, and grammar are unimportant to the clarity and precision of a written story, nor am I suggesting that writers have no need for persistence. And certainly, avid reading will help a student gain a greater sense of story. What I do want to emphasize is that the foundation of a good story's focus and design takes shape in part from what goes on in students' heads while they sit and organize their story idea, before they write a single word.

Often children write in what I call the "action-reaction mode." They get ideas for stories, perhaps even taking them from their writing folders. They begin with one action, and without planning where they might want the idea to go, they write it down in a frenzy, as if it might otherwise be lost forever. When their initial burst of creative excitement expires, they are left no option but to react to what they have written ("so a monster came and ate them"). Then they must react again ("and a bigger monster ate that monster"). I have come to believe that children—boys, in particular—have coded into their writing genes the equation: more and more exaggerated violence = action and plot. They continue escalating this "action-reaction" sequence until they must end the story, and resort to either the "pencil lift-off" or the "then I awoke" ending.

Students need to see that a story evolves out of planning, out of sitting for a while with an idea. Ouida Sebestyen offers this advice:

Sit a long time with your feet propped up and your eyes closed. Don't put pencil to paper too soon. Two thirds of writing is thinking, planning, what-if-ing, shaping in your mind what your story is going to be, what effect you mean to create, what thread or theme is going to hold everything together.

Bill Brittain says that once he has his basic plot idea, he sits down with a yellow legal pad and jots down whatever occurs to him that might work in the story. Other writers admit to using the time-honored outline in planning their stories. Stories that become something more than actions and reactions involve planning. In the classroom, I have used two common strategy worksheets to help students plan out their plots. The first is a *story sequence sheet* (see Figure 2–31). In filling out this sheet, the student pays attention to plot, characterization, introduction, setting, and climax and selects a tentative title. Once the story is mapped out, the student can "tell" the story idea (seated on the "story stool") to the class to get some early criticism and advice. At this point, the author may also take a close look at the questions written beside the boxes as guides.

The other strategy worksheet is the *story triggering sheet* (see

Figure 2–31 Story Sequence Sheet

Figure 2–32 Story Triggering Sheet

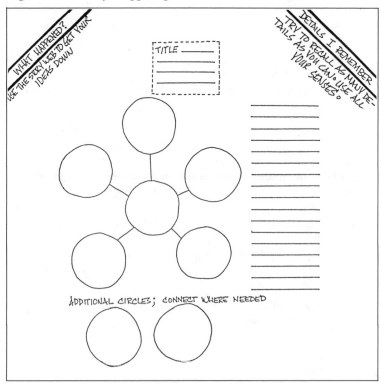

Figure 2–32). The writer jots the first idea for a story down in the center circle. It may stem from an occurrence the writer witnessed, heard of, or imagined. It may arise from meeting an odd and interesting character. It may simply be a "what if?" The student then fills in the orbiting circles with whatever further ideas the original idea triggers. The column of lines is for writing down all the details he or she can brainstorm. (At the bottom of the sheet are extra idea circles in case five are not enough.)

CONCLUSION AND CLOSING: TYING UP THE LOOSE ENDS

The end is rapidly approaching and the teller is bringing the tale to its appropriate closing. The early sense of suspense has all but subsided. A problem has found its solution. But, is the story over? Not quite. There are a couple of loose ends to tie up.

In the story of Owl, the final actions are as follows: the girl's mother takes off Owl's hat; Owl runs away; his face is revealed as he mounts his horse; the girl sees his face as handsome; Owl, not knowing, runs off, never to be seen again. Although the action of the story is now essentially over, the rising sun and Rooster's dancing allow the girl's family to see Owl's face—unfortunately for Owl. The climax, of course, is that the girl regards it as one of the most handsome faces she has ever beheld. Our expectations are now satisfied. But Owl must live with the consequences of his poor self-image.

The conclusion of the story—after the climax—is rapid. It resolves two final points: What will happen to the girl now? What about Rooster? The end.

The conclusion is a necessary part of a story. It is where the writer or storyteller tidies up everything before putting it "to bed." Think of the classic tale of Cinderella. To the astonishment of the two stepsisters, the glass slipper fits Cinderella's foot; she rightfully gains the hand of the prince. The suspense is now over, but there are still some nagging loose ends. What is to become of the cruel stepsisters? In the Arbuthnot version of the story, Cinderella forgives them, embraces them, and allows them to live in the palace with her.

The last element in many stories, particularly those that are told aloud, is the "closing," or last sentence. The closing is that ritual statement or verse that signals the audience that the story is over. It is the audience's cue to return to everyday reality, the "box of actuality." When I tell the Owl story, I bring up my hands, smile at the audience, and say gently, "The girl always hoped that he was well. And that, my friends, is the story of Owl." When I tell the Cinderella story, I can often count on the children in the audience to join me for the traditional closing: "And so Cinderella and the Prince lived. . . . " The children, of course, add the "happily ever after."

Writers often close their stories in much the same way. For example, the last words of Rudyard Kipling's *The Elephant's Child* read:

> . . . and ever since that day, O Best Beloved, all the Elephants you will ever see, besides all those that you won't, have trunks precisely like the trunk of the "satiable Elephant's Child."

In the conclusion of my tale of enchantment, "The Land Where No Light Reached," the king's daughters are freed from the belly of the giant, the two brothers and their respective brides return to rule the now-saved kingdom, and the characters know that they will need each other's abilities, strength, *and* wisdom to be successful rulers. I end the story like this:

> And so the two brothers did rule the kingdom for many, many years in both wisdom and strength.

When I talk to children about story closings I return to the metaphor of the final signpost (recall that I have described the "opening" as beginning signpost). Children need to examine the closing statements of other writers as fellow practitioners of the story-writing craft. They need to come to see how the masters do it so that they can model their efforts after them. In my writing workshops I encouraged students to write several different closing sentences for the same story and decide which one most appealed to them. One of my classroom bulletin boards has always displayed a collection of signposts containing closings from stories written by members of the class and from published books. Figure 2–33 shows several examples by first graders.

I have also encouraged my adult storytelling students to try their hands at extended poetic closings. Figure 2–34 shows a good example by Janet Johnson.

One of my favorite closings was written by a fifth-grader:

Flim, Flam, Flus
This tale's behind us.

And they lived
   happily ever after.

And she never
   returned again.

And now it is time
   to go to sleep.

Figure 2–33 Display of Closings

Figure 2–34 Poetic Closing

So now my story's ended,
and you can believe it
or not believe it.
But since you listened well
magic and luck will with you
    always dwell.

THEME: NUGGET OF A STORY'S TRUTH

Robert Frost once suggested that a poem begins in delight and ends in wisdom. The same can be said of any good story. A well-written or well-told story captures our attention and holds it through vivid characterization and the intricacies of plot. More than likely, we experience emotional satisfaction when the story's conflict is brought to some sort of resolution. For a story to have a truly lasting impact, however, it must leave us with something beyond its plot and characters—a deeper understanding, perhaps a nugget of wisdom or knowledge, something that enhances our way of thinking about people or things in the world.

This nugget of wisdom, no matter how simple or quaint it might seem or how profound it might be, is the meaning of the story, the story's theme. It is what the teller meant to say about life. Theme is what separates a funny anecdote heard at a party from a real story. A meaningful story lingers on in the mind and is stored in memory. Most of us probably cannot remember the last time we actually heard or read the biblical story of the Prodigal Son, yet the meaning of the story is still with us.

In all literature, whether folktales or modern literary masterpiece, similar themes recur. Just as chameleons change color depending on their environment, so also do stories. But no matter what color the story assumes, the wisdom within remains. Stories deal with our deepest human concerns: good and evil, friendship, self-knowledge, endurance, love, responsibility, honesty, and the value of all living things.

A theme in a story is like an unstated confirmation of a belief. We may not be able to verbalize it or even think about it consciously, but the theme connects us with an idea we are willing to accept as true. Some themes may cause us to nod our heads in agreement: "Yes, that's true. It reminds me of. . . . "Others may appear more like startling discoveries: "Hmm . . . I've never thought of it, but that's right!"

However it strikes us, the theme is the unifying reality of a story. This is the message behind the native American maxim that all stories are true, even if they never happened. The theme represents the continuity and continuation of human values. The theme might nudge us to be less self-centered, less motivated by material wealth, more compassionate. It might encourage us to believe in ourselves and our talents. It might also beckon us to live our lives more fully. I am reminded of a comment about Abraham Lincoln. According to his cousin, Dennis Hank, Abe made books tell him more than they told other people. I want my stories to tell my students as much as they can.

Being able to recognize the theme, the nugget of wisdom in a story, is a learned behavior we need to nurture. Children are creatures of the immediate, the surface: what is funny, what isn't, what tastes good, what they like. The deeper meaning of a story, beyond the action, does not automatically manifest itself to them. They are like the teenager bred in the city who looks at a mountain valley and sees merely a bunch of trees, the ground, and the sky. It takes someone who knows the valley to share its secrets: the cave where the quiet deer come to drink, the hidden, wild raspberry patch in full bloom, and the sweep of the sky when the stars come out. Children, too, need help in discerning the secrets and treasures of stories. They need teacher-mentors to guide them in discovering what lies beyond the plot line.

Through teacher modeling, examination, and class discussion children learn more sensitive reading habits. They begin to pattern their reading behavior after readers who know how to read beyond character and plot to see what a story is really about. In an interview in *Instructor* magazine, Richard C. Anderson, the director of the Center of the Study of Reading at the University of Illinois and the chief author of *Becoming a Nation of Readers,* discussed the need for teachers to draw children's attention to the deeper meaning of what they are reading. "Better comprehension of today's story," he says, "makes public the private process students ought to go through when they read tomorrow's story." Through a process of what he calls "artful questioning day after day, week after week," teachers can "expect that children will eventually internalize what it means to understand a story" (Anderson 1988, 8).

I used the *story cycle* model in my classroom and stressed the idea of looking for a nugget of truth. I encouraged students to tell their classmates something they had learned or to choose an idea they wanted to remember. Referring to the "box of actuality" and the "circle of truth," I would remind them all to carry their nugget of truth with them as they followed the path back to the actuality box. In group discussions, we would listen to each other's nuggets, and I would write them down on the blackboard. Students could also copy their nuggets on gold paper to keep in their reading folders. A sample:

From the story about Owl I want
to remember that *people shouldn't
hide their faces from others.*

When we talked together, I encouraged the children to see if their nuggets of truth could be applied to all people or all children. I would ask them, for example, if truths about dishonesty or compassion were general or if they only fit the specifics of a particular story.

I also shared my own nuggets with them:

Today we are going to reread one of my favorite stories, Millions of Cats *by Wanda Gág. But before we do, let me share one of my nuggets. I'll write it on the board:*

By caring for something, we make it most beautiful and dear to us.

Later we'll have a chance to talk about this nugget and about the ones you discover for yourselves.

After we heard the story, I might ask a few questions to encourage discussion.

- *Was my nugget demonstrated in the story?*
- *Do you think it's true? Why?*
- *Why do you think that by caring for something we might make it beautiful?*
- *How about your pets?*
- *Do you think that by caring for them—feeding and exercising them—you make them the most beautiful animals you know?*
- *Can you think of another way to say the same idea in different words?*
- *Let's write those words down.*
- *How about you—do some of you have a nugget from our story? Let's write those down too.*

As children became more experienced readers and writers, they collaborated in groups to find "theme statements" and "theme questions" in their stories. They often wrote these theme statements and questions on art paper and added an illustration. These they also kept in their reading folders. After reading *The Dancing Man* by Ruth Bornstein, one group of sixth graders identified and illustrated these themes:

- People should always follow their dreams.
- Being true to your own dream is the best.
- Can dreams come true?
- Always be true to yourself.
- Believe in and follow your dreams.
- Should people be concerned when others laugh at them?

Through modeling, collaboration, and "artful questioning," children begin to discover what they might not have seen before. This awareness comes naturally in a classroom where they are exposed to a variety of meaningful stories. They learn how to understand a story and gain access to the timeless wisdom stories hold.

THREE

STORY GAMING

At this point readers might be thinking, "OK, so those are the elements of stories and some ideas for using them, but what about *my* students with their different individual reading levels, their diverse home lives, the district's mandated use of the basal series, and the state's unrelenting use of reading skill testing?" How do we use stories in our classrooms in view of the curricular demands and constraints many of us face? In the end, it is a matter of balance. Would we throw out basals and allow only trade books in our classrooms? Would we have children read only self-chosen library books and never present new vocabulary words or assign a story from a text? Would we advocate never teaching an out-of-context, isolated reading skill, and assume that the entire class was gaining all the necessary ones and blossoming as readers simply by being in a story-saturated classroom environment? Literacy learning is far too complex an endeavor to accommodate such short-sighted notions.

We can use our basals—or not use them. They are, after all, simply collections of poems, stories, and other prose. We then balance our teaching with novels from the library, picture books, collections of stories, and anthologies of poetry. We can assign texts (with their new vocabulary words) and teach them, but we can also permit children to select and monitor their own reading materials in their reading classes: This week sports stories for Johnny and Shel Silverstein for Bonnie. We can and must identify those reading skills in which individual children need direct instruction and practice, but we also need to expose them to authentic stories simply as stories, not as vehicles for examining the rules for serial commas.

All instruction needs balance. I would never require my students to discuss and analyze the characters, setting, plot, problem, resolution, and theme of every story they read. That would take all the joy out of the finest stories—as does forcing children to read solely to answer comprehension questions. While some stories are showcases for characterization and others for theme, some ought to be enjoyed like a fine meal—simply because it tastes good. No excuses needed. The stories the children and I bring to class help me determine what types of activities to introduce. And the children themselves suggest activities that might be worthwhile and interesting with a particular story.

In my vision of a reading-writing classroom, there is a balance between teacher-directed activities and student-monitored activities, between a product-centered curriculum and experiential learning, between instruction and exploration. Reading instruction is a multifaceted endeavor involving storytelling, drama, the visual arts, writing, cooperative learning activities, puppets, flannel boards, oral reading, silent reading, readers' theater, and so on. Children learn by way of many different paths—seeing, listening, speaking, and doing. The greater the instructional variety, the richer the learning environment.

Our best language arts classrooms are not necessarily those in which whole language instruction is strictly practiced or literature-based learning advocated, nor, for that matter, are our worst classrooms the ones in which reading adheres closely to basals. Our best classrooms, in my belief, are those in which teachers incorporate the most useful of many reading methods, depending on the needs and interests of the children, in which children and teachers alike are deeply and actively engaged in the business of becoming proficient and experienced readers. These classrooms are lively arenas of literary activity and discovery.

This section will consider a number of classroom activities and ideas I have used to create and maintain a "lively literary arena." These activities are perhaps best described as "story gaming," because they are examples of learning through doing that often resemble play. Children learn by being involved in and experiencing, not simply by listening to an explanation and being tested. These activities are intended to demonstrate this idea by paying particular attention to the use of stories in the elementary classroom.

Let me add a couple of disclaimers. First, although the organization of the activities progresses from those best for primary grades to those more useful for intermediate students, this is not intended as a strict guideline. These activities have a variety of applications. What seems too juvenile for one class may be the perfect springboard for another. The sensitive teacher should try to connect the right activity with the right group of children. Second, I make no exclusive claim to any of these activities. They are the result of my years as a teacher, reader, and storyteller and most assuredly have been influenced by all I have read and seen. I intend only to suggest some strategies for implementing and organizing these kinds of activities within a classroom context and at the very least, to share some of the techniques I have found useful through the years.

PRIMARY STUDENTS: THREE Rs

For emergent readers, the most successful story material is that which entices both the eye and the ear. It offers visual and verbal images that draw children into the story and sounds and rhythms that engage their natural linguistic curiosity. The qualities of language that appeal most to young children are what reading educators are now calling the three new Rs: rhyme, rhythm, and repetition. Any story joyfully utilizing some or all of these alluring aspects of language is nearly guaranteed to be successful with youngsters. In the primary classroom story circle (either with a Big Book, a trade picture book, or a tale simply "told"), a story with rhyme, rhythm, and repetition can be the door through which young children discover the special pleasures of literature. What follows is a sampling of the story gaming activities I use in a primary classroom story circle setting.

Repetition

In delightful books such as Maurice Sendak's *Pierre* or Wanda Gág's *Millions of Cats* the lines or phrases repeated throughout the text can provide a chorus for the entire group during the telling or retelling of the stories:

> I don't care! (*Pierre*)

or

> Hundreds of cats
> Thousands of cats
> Millions and billions
>   and trillions
>   of cats (*Millions of Cats*)

With the picture book *Pierre,* I have constructed a cardboard illustration of the Pierre character with the face cut out. Individual students stand behind the cardboard, put their own faces into the cutout, and magically "become" Pierre by repeating his famous line—for countless renditions of the story. With the refrain from *Millions of Cats,* I first demonstrate and then have students join in swinging their arms right and left to the rhythm of the phrase each time it is chorused:

Hundreds of cats
   [*left hand swings to the left*]
Thousands of cats
   [*right hand swings to the right*]
Millions and billions
   [*left . . .*] [*right . . .*]
and trillions
   [*left . . .*]
of cats
   [*both left and right arms swing out simultaneously*]

Simple mime is another way to involve children in stories with repeating phrases. With *Wilfred Gordon McDonald Partridge* by Mem Fox, for example, children can act out suggested actions for each character role:

- Mrs. Jordan *playing an organ.*
- Mr. Haskin *telling a scary story.*
- Mr. Tippett *playing cricket.*
- Miss Mitchell *walking with a cane.*
- Mr. Drysdale *puffing up his chest to talk like a giant.*

Felt board (or magnetic board) stories also present opportunities to involve youngsters with the repeating story elements. For the well-known story, "The Old Woman Who Lived Alone," I have glued pictures of the parts of the story onto tagboard and attached small magnets to the back so they stick to a magnetic board.

Big big shoes.
Short short legs.
Wee wee waist.
Broad broad shoulders.
Long long arms.
Fat fat hands.
Round round head.

As the story progresses, I attach the shoes at the bottom of the board, then the legs, then the waist, and so on. As I tell the story, the children chime in with the cumulative names of body parts they see on the blackboard:

And in came two fat fat hands and fastened themselves onto those long long arms on those broad broad shoulders on that wee wee waist on those short short legs on those big big shoes.

I also use what I call *sentence boards.* These are pieces of heavy cardboard on which the words or phrases that are repeated through-out a story are printed. These *sentence boards* let students see the words they are saying. With the "The Old Woman Who Lived Alone," the three sentence boards contain these phrases:

- Come in
- Squeak
- And still she sat,
  And still she spun,
    And still she waited
      for someone to come.

Before I start, I pass the sentence boards out to three students. As I begin telling the story, I point to each child when it is his or her turn to contribute. When I say, "On that cold cold floor . . . "I point to the appropriate child, who says, "And still she sat, and still she spun, and still she waited for someone to come." That child then passes the sentence board on to another student:

I say: And as she was spinning, she heard another sound at the door, so she said . . . [*I point*]
Child says: Come in. [*passes sentence board*]
I say: Then . . . [*I point*]
Child says: Squeak. [*passes board*]

And so on.

I have also used sentence boards for the stories I have shared with slightly older students. Kipling's *The Elephant's Child,* for ex-ample, has memorable repetitions throughout the story:

- Giraffe *"with his hard, hard hoof."*
- Hippopotamus *"with her broad, broad hoof."*
- Ostrich *"with her hard, hard claw."*
- Baboon *"with his hairy, hairy paw."*
- *"Great, grey-green, greasy Limpopo River all set about with fever trees."*
- *"Vantage number 1."*

Activities such as these make it possible for even the shyest child or the least proficient reader to participate in the telling of a story. The feelings of enjoyment children experience will linger on when they return to the story as beginning readers.

Rhyme

The element of rhyme in any story provides a satisfying predictability. Children's linguistic sense often tells them what word or phrase to expect before they hear (or read) it. In the story poem "Susie Morior," for example, the last word of every other line rhymes with the one before it:

> *The fire was so hot*
> *Susie jumped in a————(pot).*
> *The pot was so black*
> *Susie dropped in a————(crack).*

Children only need to hear a couple of lines before they are supplying the words. During a story session, I pause just before the rhyming word to allow children time to guess. This procedure is referred to by language educators as "oral cloze." It allows children the opportunity to use not only picture clues (if they are available) but also their innate linguistic sense of how a rhyming story works. They then become a part of its telling.

Younger children can also create their own rhyming stories. Here's an example of a story by some second graders that is modeled after N. M. Bodecker's *Let's Marry, Said the Cherry:*

LET'S DANCE!
Said the Pants

"Let's dance," said the————. (pants)
"Yes let's," replied the————. (sweats)
"We need a note," declared the————. (coat)
"That's rocks," reported the————. (socks)
"Get down," bellowed the————. (gown)
"I'll try," perked the————. (tie)
"Not so low," warned the————. (bow)
"You might get hurt," argued the————. (shirt)
"I don't care," laughed the————. (underwear)
"Let's flip," screamed the————. (slip)
"Look at that," exclaimed the————. (hat)
"That grooves," cried the————. (shoes)
"You're too rough," complained the————. (cuff)

"Let's leave," suggested the——. (sleeve)
"I think we'd better," agreed the——. (sweater)

Another rhyming story, *Who Is Tapping at My Window?* by A. G. Deming, can be made into a small group game. The game starts with someone in the group standing up and asking the question, "Who is that tapping on my window pane?" The whole group responds, "It's not I, said the——," and individual students supply the names of rhyming sets of different animals. For example, everyone repeats, It's not I, said the——, and individual students say, cat, rat, wren, hen, fox, ox, and so on. The game ends with "It is I, said the rain, tapping at your window pane." To play the game, the leader starts with a question, the whole group answers, and the leader points to an individual for an animal (rat). The whole group repeats their line and the leader points to another individual for the rhyming animal (cat), and so on until all the rhyming animals are used up. The person with the last rhyming animal then becomes the leader, and the game starts over.

A similar game, which focuses on alliteration as well as rhyme, can be created with the universally popular *Brown Bear, Brown Bear* by Bill Martin Jr. On round pieces of tagboard, some of my older students wrote a series of alliterating extensions of Martin's well-known text (see Figure 3–1):

Hideous hedgehog, hideous hedgehog, what do you see?
  [*one student starts and hands the next circle to another student reader*]
I see a washable worm looking at me.
  [*the whole class joins in*]

Washable worm, washable worm, what do you see?
and so on with wild creations like these:

Figure 3–1 Alliterating Extension Circles

Polyvinyl polliwog.
Sea shining seagull.
Monochrome mouse.
Walloping wasp.
Hypnotized hippopotamus.
Breathtaking brontosaurus.
Monotonous mosquito.
Lilting ladybug.
Lounging leopard.
Catty-cornered camel.

To complement these rhyming activities, a number of rhyming narrative poems are available in a picture book format that is particularly rewarding to share with younger children in the story circle. Some of my favorites are Dr. Seuss, of course, A. A. Milne, and Ogden Nash. Anthologies of story poems and other books in the children's section of the library offer further possibilities.

Rhythm

In my story programs I include activities to illustrate the rhythmic patterns of stories. These I call my "snap, clap, and slap" stories because they are ideal for the snapping of fingers, clapping of hands, and slapping of legs during the telling. The nursery rhyme "Higglety Pigglety Pop" offers an easy example:

Higglety	Pigglety	Pop
[clap hands]	*[slap legs]*	*[clap hands and freeze]*

The dog	has eaten	the mop
[clap hands]	*[slap legs]*	*[clap hands and freeze]*

By clapping and slapping, children feel the lively pulse of words in their rhythmic patterns and bring to the printed page a spirit of playfulness. Another rhyming chant entitled "We Must," which my wife wrote to use with her first graders, follows this same pattern.

When	we're	sit	'ting	in	the	class
[slap legs]	*[clap hands]*	*[slap]*	*[clap]*	*[slap]*	*[clap]*	*[snap fingers twice]*

We	must	ne/ver	fuss	or	sass
[slap]	*[clap]*	*[slap/ clap]*	*[slap]*	*[clap]*	*[snap twice]*

With pieces like this, she found it best to teach the snap-clap-snap pattern first, then add the words orally, and only then present the printed version of the poem. Her goal was to have the children feel and hear the rhythm before they responded to the print. She wrote the poem on long sheets of butcher paper attached at the top to a hanger which could be hung up in her room (see Figure 3–2.)

Figure 3–2 Coat Hanger Display for a Clap/Snap Poem

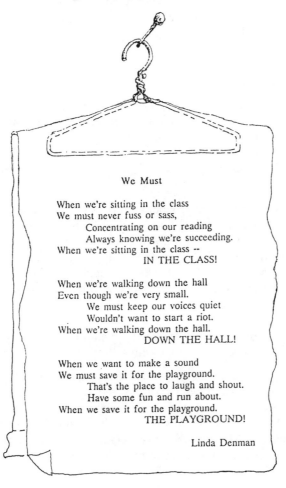

We Must

When we're sitting in the class
We must never fuss or sass,
    Concentrating on our reading
    Always knowing we're succeeding.
When we're sitting in the class --
       IN THE CLASS!

When we're walking down the hall
Even though we're very small.
    We must keep our voices quiet
    Wouldn't want to start a riot.
When we're walking down the hall.
       DOWN THE HALL!

When we want to make a sound
We must save it for the playground.
    That's the place to laugh and shout.
    Have some fun and run about.
When we save it for the playground.
       THE PLAYGROUND!

       Linda Denman

Experiencing exciting books that seem to revel in the delights of rhyme, rhythm, and repetition encourages children to read the same books independently. They can ponder the pictures, sing the refrains, and clap out the rhythms, mimicking the experience of the story circle. Along the way, they come to understand that books are made up of covers, titles, and pages. They soon recognize that printed words are separated by spaces, that words have a letter-sound relationship and move from left to right in a line and from top to bottom on a page. They discover that marks of punctuation are clues to the pacing of stories. Their fluency with the text grows naturally through continuous practice. As their familiarity and fluency develop, phrasing and expression replace letter-by-letter, word-by-word decoding. Children who can read these first books smoothly and comfortably will be eager members of the world of books and readers.

STORY SENSE

Full membership in the world of books and readers extends beyond the knowledge of the characteristics of print. It also grows as children become better able to predict the nature of the story inside the book. Sitting on my "story stool" holding up a new book to share with a group of primary students, I might begin with questions like these:

- By looking at the cover, what kind of story should we expect to hear today? Why? What clues did you find?
- Does the title suggest a problem of some sort?
- Who is the author? Do we know any other books by the same person? What type of books does he or she normally write?
- What characters would you expect in a book like this?
- Here are some of the pictures in the book. When and where might you assume the story takes place? What kind of mood or feeling do the pictures create? Let's read the author's opening and see if we get any other clues about the setting of the story.

After we heard the story, we would compare some of our initial predictions with what we had discovered in the text. By rehearsing this process orally in the story circle, young readers soon take themselves through the same process mentally before they read a book independently. They discover that reading is an ongoing process of predictions and confirmation or revision of those predictions.

Any prediction about a story before or during reading is predicated on a sense of the structure of that story. As we have seen, stories often conform to certain conventions in much the same way that sentences conform to identifiable patterns. What I call "story sense" develops in young readers through repeated exposure to the organizational framework of stories—essentially through learning how stories are put together. Many of my story gaming activities are intended to demonstrate these patterns. The ancient storyteller's stick is one example.

> There is a storytelling custom which involves an intricately carved wooden walking staff called a "storytelling stick." While a pre-literate storyteller told a story, he would hold his "storytelling stick" and lightly touch the carvings, slowly moving his fingers down the length of the staff. His fingers would be touching embedded carvings, which served as reminders for him of the sequence, characters, and episodes of the story he was telling. These sticks are examples of early memory devices used by storytellers before the invention of print. They helped the ancient storytellers remember their tales in the same way that rosary beads help Roman Catholic priests count and recite certain prayers. (Denman 1986, 4)

This custom came to my mind a while back as I was preparing a presentation for a class. I was struck by the fact that the storyteller's stick accomplishes for the storyteller what a *semantic map* does for beginning readers. A semantic map, drawn either on the blackboard or on paper, demonstrates the structure of the story and the relationship of the parts to the whole. It captures the flow and the evolving order of the major story happenings and helps organize ideas for young readers even before they begin to read the story. And as Frank Smith points out, comprehension is inseparably linked to what exists in the mind of the reader prior to and during the act of reading (Smith 1985, 72–91).

Combining the theory of semantic mapping and the idea of the storyteller's stick, I made a large mobile out of cardboard shapes— triangles, rectangles, and circles—fastened together with pipe cleaners (see Figure 3–3). I used the mobile with the story "A Single Grain of Rice," which, briefly, goes like this:

> A king calls his four daughters together and explains that he is going away and that they are to rule the kingdom in his absence. Before he leaves, he gives each of them a single grain of rice and tells them to "do the best you can" with the rice and to be prepared to show him their grains of rice if he

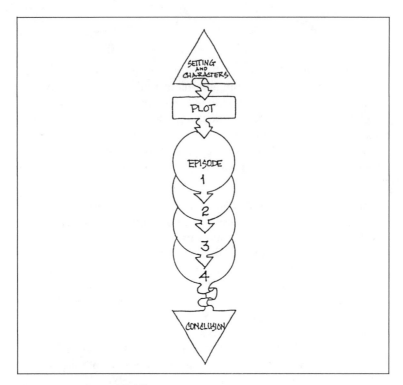

Figure 3–3 Story Mobile

should return. Each daughter does something different with her rice, trying to comply with the father's order. Many years later, the king returns, quite old by this time, and asks to see the rice. Each daughter gives her father a grain of rice except for the last, who no longer has the original grain. She has planted it and watched it multiply into many fine rice fields. The fourth daughter, of course, has done the very best and receives the king's crown. (Simms 1981)

The mobile allows me to talk about the structure of the story and point out the relationship of the individual episodes to the whole. It makes it easy for children to see that each circle represents what one of the daughters did with the rice. I also talk about story elements (setting, character, plot, episodes, conclusion). Having the youngsters hold up the mobile, I encourage them to retell the story by following the shapes, as if using a storyteller's stick.

As a writing exercise, children can create a different version of the story by changing the gender of the characters, their individual actions, and the eventual outcome but leaving the structure of the story intact. In my files, I have some wonderful versions written by fifth-graders. One student had a king give each of his daughters a hug and tell them to do the best they could with it. Another had a father give each of his sons five notes of music. A mother in another version gave her daughters each a box of kindness, in another, the power of courage, and in yet another, half a story. Students can use a *story mobile sheet* (see Figure 3–4) as a planning aid in this

Figure 3–4 Story Mobile Sheet

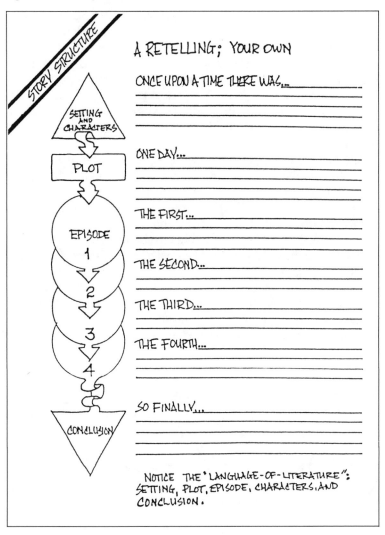

STORY STRUCTURE

SETTING AND CHARACTERS

PLOT

EPISODE 1
2
3
4

CONCLUSION

A RETELLING; YOUR OWN

ONCE UPON A TIME THERE WAS..._____

ONE DAY..._____

THE FIRST..._____

THE SECOND..._____

THE THIRD..._____

THE FOURTH..._____

SO FINALLY..._____

NOTICE THE "LANGUAGE-OF-LITERATURE":
SETTING, PLOT, EPISODE, CHARACTERS, AND
CONCLUSION.

writing assignment. With a group of younger students the story can be dramatized using hand-held road signs (see p. 56) for the "Once upon a time," "One day," "The first," "The second," "The third," "The fourth," and "So, finally." Each child can tell one part of the story.

Techniques such as semantic mapping or the use of a story mobile also help beginning readers to sense that there is an overall structure to a story. As with the rising-falling action triangle (p. 55), they see that stories are not simply random, like balls bouncing down through a pinball machine, but that they follow a design.

"A Single Grain of Rice" is an example of a simple, sequential story characterized by a setting (a kingdom), a problem (the best choice of actions with the grain of rice), and a series of separate events (the daughters' actions) leading to a resolution of the problem (the fourth daughter receiving the crown). Anticipating how the father will respond to each of the daughter's choices creates narrative tension. This same story could have been illustrated with the rising/falling action model (see p. 55) or the story sequence sheet (see p. 60).

Another recurring pattern in folktales and children's stories involves a cumulative succession of events. The popular rhyme *The Poor Old Lady Who Swallowed a Fly* by Rose Bonne is an excellent example. The old lady swallows a fly, and then a spider to catch the fly, a bird, a cat, a dog, a cow, and a horse.

Young children will see the cumulative building effect of this type of story if you illustrate it on the blackboard with a series of enlarging circles (see Figure 3–5).

Using the idea of enlarging circles, I sometimes have children take the old story, "The Pancake" (found in many folktale anthologies), and create a *circle book.* In this story, a woman bakes a pancake for her family, and in asking for a bit of cake, each of her seven children adds a compliment to the request:

Figure 3–5 Cumulative Story Illustration

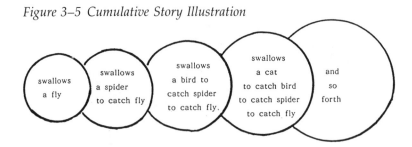

First child: "Oh give me a bit of the pancake, mother dear, I am so hungry."
Second child: "Oh darling mother dear . . ."
Third child: "Oh darling, good mother . . ."
Fourth child: "Oh darling, good, nice mother . . ."
Fifth child: "Oh darling, pretty, good, nice mother . . ."
Sixth child: "Oh darling, pretty, good, nice, clever mother . . ."
Seventh child: "Oh darling, pretty, good, nice, clever, sweet mother . . ."

The mother finally agrees to give all of them a bit of the pancake when it is done, but the pancake overhears, jumps from the pan, and rolls away. With the mother and children pursuing, the pancake rolls on until it meets a man who asks if the pancake will stop so he can eat it. The pancake replies, "Well, I have given the slip to the Goody Poody (the woman) and the Good Man and the seven squalling children. I may well slip through your fingers, Manny Panny." The pancake rolls on until it meets a hen (Henny Penny) who again asks if it will stop. The pancake's answer starts with the same cumulating list, "Well, I have given the slip to the Goody Poody and the Good Man and the seven squalling children and Manny Panny. I may well slip through your claws, Henny Penny." In each new encounter—with Cocky Locky, Ducky Lucky, Goosey Poosey, and Piggy Wiggy,—the list is repeated and added to.

As it turns out, the pig (Piggy Wiggy) convinces the pancake to cross a stream by riding on her snout—and eats it.

Starting with a small circle, children write the first statement of the cumulative list ("Oh mother dear . . ."). Then, on a slightly larger circle, they write the next statement ("Oh darling mother dear . . ."). By the time the circles reach the list of animals, they are large enough to write the words (a man, a hen, a rooster, and so on) and illustrate them. The last circle, the largest, contains the final statement. Once all the circles are fastened with a ring into a circle book, (see Figure 3–6) children can tell the story and show the pictures from the story stool.

Another recurring story pattern is the *quest story.* Simply put, a quest story follows a chronological time progression in which a character sets out to reach a goal and the episodes along the way form a life-journey. In Tomie de Paola's *The Clown of God,* for example, readers first meet Giovanni as a small boy who can juggle and follow him until his death as an old man. Within the story, Giovanni's juggling act forms a recurring episode at each stage of his life. In Ruth Bornstein's *The Dancing Man,* Joseph begins in his

Figure 3–6 Circle Story

home village and dances across his homeland from village to village into his old age.

In working with quest stories, I often have children do what I call a *story journey map*. They draw the episodes of the character's life along a path, starting at the beginning of the story, thus mapping out, according to their own design, the plot line of the story. Figure 3–7 shows an example of a story journey map for *The Dancing Man*.

The story journey map shows the events in Joseph's life in chronological order. Children can use these maps as mnemonic *telling sheets*, when they retell the story in their own words.

Children develop a "sense of story" through engaging activities with simple, predictable story structures. They internalize these structures and come to recognize them as the recurring shapes and patterns that stories have. As they begin to read or hear an unfamiliar story that conforms to one of these patterns, they fit new information from the story into their previous story pattern. In this way they gain an organizational foundation for understanding as they read.

RETELLINGS

Children's enjoyment of a story and their understanding of it are enhanced if they have an opportunity to retell it. In my classroom, the story stool in the story circle served as the speaker's platform

Figure 3–7 Story Journey Map

for the telling or innovative retelling of stories. I developed several story gaming activities to facilitate this.

With primary children, a simple story with only a few characters, such as Shel Silverstein's *The Giving Tree,* can be used in game-playing fashion. First, the story is shared a number of times, either by reading the book aloud or telling the story in story circle. Often, the follow-up discussion focuses on the chronological pattern of the story: young boy, teenager, adult, old man, very old man. The life cycle of the tree in the story can also be mapped out: loss of leaves and apples, loss of branches, loss of trunk, stump. Children's drawings of the characters at different stages can be glued onto individual pieces of tagboard, making *story board characters.* Spreading these pictures of the characters out on the floor, children move them around to act out the story while they tell it in their own words.

A similar imaginative retelling can be done with Maurice Sendak's *Where the Wild Things Are.* Children first draw pictures of Max, the Wild Things, his boat, and the waiting dinner. Then, they mix the pictures up and put their story-making imaginations to work. After looking at their *Wild Things* pictures, the Kindergarten students of one of my graduate students told this story, transcribed here from the oral telling:

JAMES

Once upon a time lived a little boy named James who lived in Hawaii. James was in the boat and the boat was rocking. He was getting ready to fall out of the boat. He might fall into the water—the deep water. James saw a monster, and the monster crawled into the water and caught James. The monster took James to the monsters' castle where all of the other monsters lived. At the castle, James put on the queen's hat and tried to scratch the monster. The monster tried to run away because the monster was scared. The monster said, "STOP! GET AWAY FROM ME!"

Then, James climbed up the tree to catch the mama monster. He hit the mama monster with his hat (crown). James didn't know what to do so he got out of the castle and ran away. He broke the door, and the queen monster was mad! She (the queen) got her daughter, Princess Aurora, and Princess Aurora went into the room and got a stick and hit James—but James didn't care. That didn't hurt James.

The monsters were doing some things that were good— like sharing food with each other, pineapples and fruit, and sharing swings. The monsters were good and nice to James now and they became friends.

James decided to go home and get ready for his DELICIOUS AND NUTRITIOUS dinner—of apples, soup and milk. James wanted to go back to the woods to get the monsters and the queen, to bring back to his home.

In working with third- and fourth-grade students to learn to retell simple stories, I occasionally lined up the *Wild Things* pictures they had drawn in a row, following the sequence in the book. I then added sentence boards for the spoken parts of the story:

"I'll eat you up."
"Be still!"
"Let the wild rumpus begin."
"Now stop!"
"No!"

Students then retold the story in their own words, incorporating the exact words Max says in the story. This gave them a chance to work with voice characterization (how Max would sound saying the words) in their telling.

Some stories present youngsters with the opportunity to create a *parallel story journey map.* Using this map, students chart the events in a story and create an imaginative parallel retelling. A group of second graders took Arnold Lobel's "The Garden" and wrote a parallel story, "Toad Learns to Read." Figure 3–8 shows their map and how the points in each story (written out) correspond.

Another retelling activity for older students is to have them choose a story and create a *skeleton outline* of it. They write short notes of the story's happenings (with little detail or embellishment) on three-by-five-inch index cards, stack the cards in the correct sequence, and "tell" the story from the story stool with only the cards to help them. Figure 3–9 shows an example of a skeleton outline on a story sequence sheet for Leo Tolstoy's tale, "The King and the Shirt."

Using these cards, the students can embellish the story with re-membered details. For example, a child might "tell" the fourth card in this way:

> Everyone complained of wanting something. If they were rich, they were sick and wanted health. If they were healthy, they were poor and wanted wealth. If they were healthy and rich, they had bad wives . . . and so on. Nowhere could a truly happy man be found.

Many books can be adapted for what I call a *pass reading.* This involves a book and a handful of index cards on which are written selections from the book (for example, the words one of the characters said), which are attached with paper clips to the appropriate pages of the book. From the story stool, a student begins reading the book. When a page with an index card on it comes up, the student passes the card to someone in the audience to read. A book easily adapted for a "pass-reading" is Dr. Seuss's immortal *Green Eggs and Ham.* The words that the character "Sam-I-am" asks in the story (i.e., "Would you like them here or there?") can be written out on index cards and paper clipped to the corresponding pages in the book for a student to pass out during his or her reading.

A whole reading group can also be involved with the making of a story by using a *story wheel.* I adapted the story wheel from an activity conceived by Norma Livo (co-author of *Storytelling Process and Practice*). It consists of a story written in a circle with fifteen blanks (Figure 3–10). There are eight to ten possible words for each blank written on index cards (see Figure 3–11 for a sample of some of the cards I have used to accompany the wheel). Each of fifteen students has a card. Using the wheel, one child starts the story by reading "There once was a————" and then points to the person

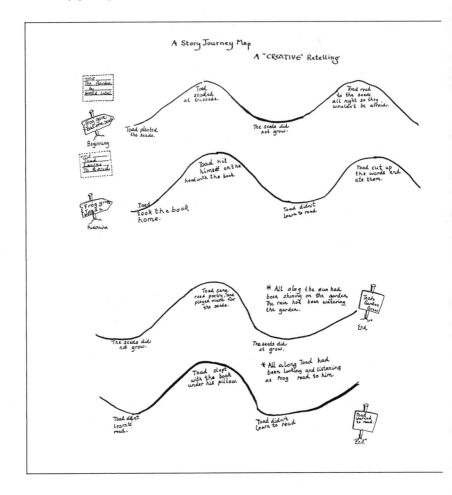

with card #1. That person supplies a word from his or her card. The leader continues reading up to the next blank and points to the person with card #2, who supplies a word from his or her list. The leader continues all the way through the story wheel. A new story is created every time the wheel is used.

As an extension of this activity, children can go through the story twice, the first time to create the story and the second to rehearse how the story should sound being told. For example, I might ask, "How would a storyteller say 'horrible scoundrel' or 'helpless hermit' in a story?" Children can practice a variety of vocal expressions and then tell the story a second time with much greater vocal effect in their renditions. Here are some examples of words from the story wheel that students learn to express as a storyteller might:

Parallel Story Journey Mapping

Title:

The Garden by Arnold Lobel

Opening:

Frog gave Toad some seeds

Sequence of actions:

1. Toad planted the seeds
2. Toad shouted at the seeds
   The seeds did not grow
3. Toad read to the seeds all
   night so they won't be afraid
   The seeds did not grow
4. Toad sang, read poetry, and
   played music for the the seeds
   The seeds did not grow
5. But all along, the sun had been
   shining on the garden. The
   rain had been watering
   the garden

Closing:

The seeds began to grow

Title:

Toad Learns to Read by second graders

Opening:

Frog gave Toad a book

Sequence of actions:

1. Toad took the book home
2. Toad hit himself on the head
   with the book
   Toad didn't learn to read
3. Toad cut up the words and
   ate them
   Toad didn't learn to read
4. Toad slept with the book
   under his pillow
   Toad didn't learn to read
5. But all along, Toad had been
   listening to Frog read to him

Closing:

Toad learned to read

Figure 3–8 Parallel Story Journey Map

grizzly
hideous
ghastly
monstrous
joyfully
meagerly
murky
dreary
laughing at
tortured
wretched
pathetic

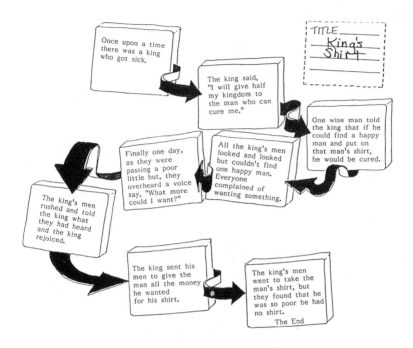

Figure 3–9 Skeleton Outline of a Story

Working in tandem, intermediate students can prepare a *two-voice story* on their own. I conceived this idea after seeing a re-markable tandem storytelling duo, "The Folktellers"—two women who tell stories together, each taking the role of a different character. I would take a short story, such as "Cookies" by Arnold Lobel, and have the students select the part of either Frog or Toad. After ex-perimenting with voice characterizations, rehearsing simple ges-tures, and practicing a little, they do the story for the class. Another excellent example of a simple story for two voices is the old anecdote-story "No News" (the version I use was told by Nat M. Willis and is found in the *Sounds of Language* series). The story is a conversation between a man returning home after being away for a much-needed rest and his servant Henry, who meets him at the train depot with news from home. Two eager students—one taking the man's part, the other that of the servant Henry—can easily adapt this into a hilarious tandem telling.

A final example of a story gaming activity involves the use of *picture boards*. Intermediate students often want to try telling a story

Figure 3–10 Story Wheel

Figure 3–11 Sample Cards for Story Wheel

Figure 3–12 Sample of a Student's Picture Board

using a dialect different from their own. When they find a story they like, they create a series of picture boards for each of the characters on standard-size pieces of tagboard or cardboard. On the reverse side, the students write down significant pieces of spoken dialogue they want to include in their telling. By holding their picture boards so as to conceal the written words from the audience, they can read the words or use them as cues, glancing down as they progress through the story. For example, a fifth grader in one of my classes decided to use the Appalachian story *"The Old Sow and the Three Shoats"* (the Southern version of *"The Three Pigs"*) collected by Richard Chase in his book *Grandfather Tales*. Figure 3–12 shows a reproduction of one of his picture boards. On the back of the picture board of the red fox, the student had written these snatches of dialect to use in his telling:

> "Oo, no, little piggy! Rocks and bricks'll be awful cold. Why, you'uld freeze! Build you house out of chips and cornstalks."

> "By the beard on my chin, I'll blow your house in."

Using the picture boards like a picture book, he remembered the story line of his telling but referred to his notes whenever he was having the character speak. The written notes served as a security blanket (or cheat sheet) while he performed.

Involving children in these and other story gaming activities opens the door to other ways of exploring language. Stories become not just words printed on pages but texts that can be creatively manipulated and brought to life through voice, facial expression, and gesture. In the last few years of my classroom teaching I organized a storytelling club for interested older students. We learned a lot together. Since then, I have spoken to many groups of young storytellers. What I have discovered is that student storytellers learn best through demonstration. They learn to tell stories by hearing many stories told, by being led through a storyteller's preparation of a story, and by being coached in their efforts. An activity I always include with groups of beginning storytellers is one in which I tell a story and then pass out a copy of the same story and take them through a behind-the-scenes look at how I prepare.

Using *"The Tiger's Whisker,"* from *The Tiger's Whisker and Other Tales from Asia and the Pacific* by Harold Courlander, for example, I show students how I "map out" the story, as I learn it (see Figure 3–13).

I explain that, with this particular story, I need to remember and organize in my head what Yun Ok does each night on the mountain in order to gain the confidence of the tiger:

> From a safe distance, she held out food and called the tiger to come and eat.
>
> ⬇
>
> Each night, she did the same thing, but moved a few steps closer to his cave.
>
> ⬇
>
> Finally, she got close enough to speak in a soft, soothing voice.
>
> ⬇
>
> She got so close she could stand in front of the tiger and hold a bowl out to him.
>
> ⬇
>
> She was close enough to rub his head gently with her hand.
>
> ⬇
>
> On the last night, caressing the tiger's head, she spoke to him and gently snipped one of his whiskers.

I also write out on a three-by-five-inch index card the hermit's climactic comments to the young woman, so I can memorize them and use them word-for-word in my telling. Finally, I consider how I will use my hands to show the young woman holding out the bowl of rice, rubbing the tiger's head, and finally snipping the whisker, and I practice these gestures.

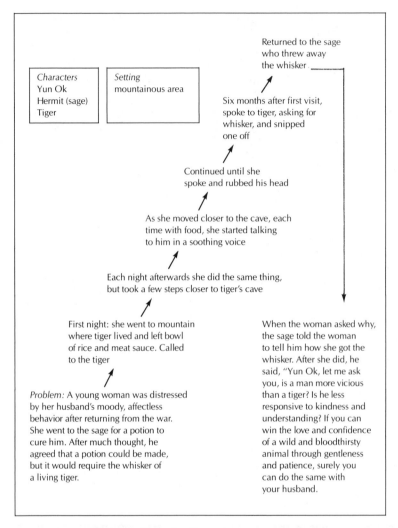

Returned to the sage
who threw away
the whisker

Six months after first visit,
spoke to tiger, asking for
whisker, and snipped
one off

Continued until she
spoke and rubbed his head

As she moved closer to the cave, each
time with food, she started talking
to him in a soothing voice

Each night afterwards she did the same thing,
but took a few steps closer to tiger's cave

First night: she went to mountain
where tiger lived and left bowl
of rice and meat sauce. Called
to the tiger

Characters
Yun Ok
Hermit (sage)
Tiger

Setting
mountainous area

Problem: A young woman was distressed
by her husband's moody, affectless
behavior after returning from the war.
She went to the sage for a potion to
cure him. After much thought, he
agreed that a potion could be made,
but it would require the whisker of
a living tiger.

When the woman asked why,
the sage told the woman
to tell him how she got the
whisker. After she did, he
said, "Yun Ok, let me ask
you, is a man more vicious
than a tiger? Is he less
responsive to kindness and
understanding? If you can
win the love and confidence
of a wild and bloodthirsty
animal through gentleness
and patience, surely you
can do the same with
your husband.

Figure 3–13 Mapping Out of a Story

Here are some guidelines I hand out to my beginning student storytellers:

• Choose a story that appeals to you, one that you really like and want to spend some time with.
• Read it over and over (out loud if it is appropriate). Try to gain a feel for the flow of the author's words, the motivation of the characters, the setting and structure of the story.

- Employ some strategy for organizing the story (in your mind or on paper)—story sequence sheet, story skeleton cards, rising/falling action model, drawn out mobile—whatever suits the story and works best for you.
- Visualize the specifics of the story's setting as clearly as you can. See the dimensions of the house in the story or the flow of the stream that needs to be crossed.
- Make sentence boards for the memorable phrases you want to use word-for-word in your telling (rhymes, important sentences, descriptions, opening and closing).
- Tell the story out loud to hear how it sounds. Use a tape recorder if you like. Make adjustments if you need to. Write yourself notes. Notice what gestures you use naturally when you tell it. Decide if you want to continue to use them or to add some more.
- Spend time with your characters; think about them. Try to analyze how they feel, speak, behave. Consider a variety of facial expressions. See if you can find an experience in your own life that is similar to one of theirs (good or bad).
- Finally, think about some of the finer techniques of storytelling, dialect, vocal control, or dramatization. Use only what works. Rehearse your story's three "Ps": *phrasing, pausing,* and *pacing.*

As children prepared their stories, I coached them on what I call the "behind the words work" and talked about what made one telling more successful than another:

- *Visualization.* Close your eyes and focus on each scene in the story. The more clearly you picture it in your head, the more tangible it becomes to the audience. See different scenes or settings as "picture units." Map each picture unit in your head.
- *Vocal work.* Listen to the telling. Don't worry about the author's grammatical structure, unless you want to use it to your advantage. As you rehearse and listen to yourself, emphasize vital words. Take a role; become a character. Imagine that the story will bring joy to an audience. Enjoy the sound of your own voice. Consider appropriate inflection (changes within a single word) and intonation (changes within a line or phrase). Train yourself to pace your telling in a variety of ways.
- *Gestures and facial expressions.* Analyze your gestures and facial expressions. Use a mirror, if you think it will help you. Do they add to or detract from a smooth telling? Are they meaningful to the content of the story? Rehearse those you use until they appear "natural."

Through exposure, demonstration, coaching, and, of course, practice, students of all ages can become excellent storytellers. In my classroom, the once teacher-dominated story sessions exploded into lively, student-directed storytelling. Dramatic readings, tandem telling, readers' theater, and story gaming activities replaced workbooks and comprehension exercises. Once the door was open to student-involved storytelling, it was impossible to close . . . and some of the skills sheets and workbook pages gathered dust on the shelves.

ENLIVENING CLASSROOM ROUTINES

Earlier I described the most successful reading classrooms as lively arenas of literary learning and discovery. Much of a classroom's liveliness, I believe, is results from the use of a wide array of story gaming activities. The concerns, of course, are how do teachers manage activities like those I have described? How do they incorporate self-selection of reading material and activities and, at the same time, monitor individual students' reading progress? Clearly, it is much easier to gauge the progress of one or two reading groups reading the same story, quietly writing out answers to a series of comprehension questions, and filling in workbooks. It is equally dull, if continued day after day.

Many teachers are finding that individual reading folders, reading conferences, and learning centers are useful aids in classroom organization, and I will sketch how I have used them with respect to stories. It is important to realize, however, that there is no step-by-step procedure for creating a lively classroom. When children and teachers learn together, it simply happens. It's unavoidable. In my own classroom, we used basal selections, had group lessons on an isolated skill with an overhead projector, and still found time for a variety of story gaming activities in whole class and individual reading groups. Some weeks we would be working in small groups and other weeks, individually. Some days we would be reading; some days, writing; most days, both. Sometimes individual students would be working at the learning center; sometimes a learning center activity would be assigned to a group of students. On some occasions, students selected activities to use with a story; on other occasions, I did the selecting. Every year was different from the year before and every month different, in varying degrees, from the month before.

To keep track of all this, my intermediate students kept reading folders in which was recorded what was read, the dates, and the activities (assigned or selected) they completed. Along with these records, the folders also contained reading logs for written responses to what the students were reading. In individual reading conferences, students discuss with me their reactions to the stories they were reading. Although these conferences varied in length as well as in direction and focus, I hoped to accomplish three things each time I held a reading conference:

- I wanted to make sure I listened to the children and allowed them to respond in their own way to what they were reading. I wanted to give them time to discuss any activities they might want to pursue with a particular book. I also wanted to give each child a chance to read aloud a "selected moment" from his or her book.
- I wanted to ask questions of the children—wide-open questions that allowed them to demonstrate their literary knowledge: What can you tell me about the author's style? What were the book's strengths and/or weaknesses? How do you think the author went about writing this book?
- I wanted to set the stage for a continuation of the children's reading by suggesting another book or letting them know what other books their classmates were enjoying. I might encourage them to write to the author of their book. I might even steer them into some fiction writing of their own.

Toward a Reading-Writing Classroom by Andrea Butler and Jan Turbill has an extensive list of appropriate questions to use in conferences for different story genres—fantasy stories, mystery stories, school stories, family stories, biographies, and adventure stories. I highly recommend their book to you.

Along with completed assignments, book critiques, personal reading inventories,* story sheets, theme cards, art projects—whatever we were producing in class—were included in the reading folders. I reviewed students' folders on a regular basis to get a sense of their progress. Many other teachers I have met have designed and used similar folders to correspond to the organization and expectations of their own reading classrooms.

---

*Reading inventories were simply a list of interests that a child might draw on in selecting reading materials. The lists included pets, hobbies, sports, personal experiences, ambitions, favorite authors, favorite types of stories, places where the student had lived, places he or she would want to live, occupations of parents and guardians, and so on.

My classroom also included several story learning centers with activities students could pursue either individually or with a partner. Sometimes these were activities I used year after year; other times they were inspired by the interest of the students or by my recognition that a reading skill needed a bit of practice. Here is a sample of some I used.

Character guessing

A game I used from time to time was called *character guessing*. A student selects the name of a familiar story character from a plastic bag containing a number of them written on pieces of tagboard and pins it to the back of another student. That student tries to guess who he or she is by asking a series of questions that can be answered only by a "yes" or a "no." For example,

- Am I from a fictional story?
- Am I from a realistic fiction story?
- Am I a human character?
- Am I a good character?
- Am I a bad character?
- Am I a character from the present?
- Am I a character from the past?
- Am I a character in the future?
- Am I an animal character?

A variation of this type of character guessing game is one where a student chooses a familiar character and writes "one-phrase answers" to the following five questions:

1. How does he/she look?
2. How does he/she act?
3. How does he/she speak?
4. How does he/she feel?
5. How does he/she appear to others?

The answers are then presented to the class for them to guess which character the student was writing about. Here are some sample answers for Arnold from Steven Kellogg's picture book, *Can I Keep Him?*

1. Like a yellow-haired little kid.
2. Caringly, and curious about all animals.
3. Questioning, questioning, questioning.

4. Lonely for a friend or pet.
5. At times, annoyingly.

Other story gaming activities that many teachers use involve having the children write imaginary conversations for characters. Students can create some interesting dialogues between

- The character and the book's author.
- The reader and the character.
- The reader and the author.
- Two characters in the same book.
- Two characters (or more) from more than one book.

In the same vein, children can interview a story's character (supplying supposed answers); write a letter to or from a book's character; or write an evaluation of a character suggesting how that character might have behaved differently. Students can also compare a story character to a real person.

Story sequencing

At another learning center, I set up a sequencing activity. A number of simple stories are divided into segments and mixed up. Working in pairs, students try to put each story in the correct sequence. On the written guidelines, I encourage students to trust their "sense of story" and to watch carefully for authors' word clues ("once upon a time," "after that," "finally," "next," "then").

Themes

A learning center activity involving themes asked students to take a series of picture books and write theme statements and questions for them. For example, for the book *Rosie and Michael* by Judith Viorst, one student wrote this theme statement and question:

There are many qualities involved in being a good friend.
What does it take to be a friend?

The student then took out key words, leaving blanks:

There are many———involved in being a good———.
What does it———to be a———?

The sentences with the blanks are then attached with a paper clip to the book. The object of the activity is to have other classmates read the book and try to fill in the blanks from their understanding of the story's theme. Here are a few more examples:

THE SPOOKY TAIL OF PREWITT PEACOCK

BY BILL PEET

Don't (_judge_) people by the way they (_look_).
Why is it (_important_) to treat all (_people_) the same—regardless
of how they (_look_)?

OLIVER BUTTON IS A SISSY

BY TOMIE DE PAOLA

It's (_best_) to work at the (_abilities_) and (_interests_) you have.
How do you (_handle_) peers who make (_fun_) of you?

HATTIE AND THE FOX

BY MEM FOX

People should take (_warnings_) or advice to (_heart_).
Why is it that (_people_) don't listen to good (_advice_)?

Leads

A number of opening passages from books and stories may be
gathered and typed on a discussion sheet for use in still another
learning center. Children team up, read the passages, and speculate
about what may happen in the story. Afterwards, they read the story
or, if possible, listen to it on a tape.

To help students get started with this activity, I give them some
questions to get them thinking:

From the lead, who do you suppose the story's characters are? Do
you have any sense from the lead of the characters' natures?
What problem is hinted at in the lead?
How might that problem be resolved? Don't be too specific—an-
swer in general terms.

Figure 3–14 shows the thoughts of several students after they read
the opening of Arlene Mosel's story, _Tikki Tikki Tembo_.
The students' speculation:

We think that since it started "Once upon a time," whatever
happens, the story will end happily. Probably a second son
feels bad since his name is so short, and he has to prove

Figure 3–14 Discussion Sheet for Leads

himself. Maybe he outdoes the first son or maybe saves him from danger or something. We bet that at the end of the story the second son gets a long name.

Closings

In a similar way, story closings can inspire learning activities. After reading a closing, students must guess what might have occurred during the course of the story. They are then given the opportunity to listen to a recorded version of the story (see Figure 3–15 for a sample of the blank learning center sheet I have used with this activity).

Titles

The titles given to stories sometimes have very interesting origins. A good title is not always easy to find. Sandy Asher, a prolific writer, says what coming up with the right title is to her:

I think of wonderful titles and no story to go with them, or I write stories and can't find titles to go with them. Sometimes I

Figure 3–15 Discussion Sheet for Closings

make lists of all possibilities—serious and silly—and my husband picks and chooses among them to come up with the final title.

Other writers say they leave the titles up to their editors. At any rate, challenging students to think of good titles can inspire interesting learning center activities. One is to have small groups of students go to the library and take one shelf of books each. Then as a group they look at all the titles on that shelf and choose the top ten. They analyze why those titles are more effective in comparison with the others and report their findings to the whole class. They may find it effective to present these findings on a sheet similar to the one in Figure 3–16.

Here is what some fifth graders decided when they did this survey.

"We liked these titles [*On Your Own, Jonathan Down Under, The Incredible Journey, Blubber,* and *Indian in the Cupboard*] because they brought on our curiosity. Titles like *On Your Own, Jonathan Down Under,* and *The Incredible Journey* sounded like a mystery so it caught our attention. Titles like *Blubber* and *Indian in the Cupboard* suggested something

weird and funny so we were interested.
"The other titles [*Peter Pan, The Wicked Stepdog, Miss Hickory,* and *Chip Has Many Brothers*] we didn't like. They sounded juvenile and did not intrigue us at all. *The Wicked Stepdog* sounded dumb. We don't think we would pick up a book with a title like that. The title about Chip having many brothers sounded like a real boring story. A book about someone named Miss Hickory didn't interest us at all."

Another activity asks students to take a book and create alternative titles for it. As a guideline I suggested that they try to think of

- Something that captures the reader's attention.
- Something short enough to be memorable.
- Something pronounceable.

Figure 3–16 Title Study Sheet

Titles

Best   Worst

_____   _____
_____   _____
_____   _____
_____   _____

Generalized results

_____
_____
_____
_____

Team members

_____
_____
_____
_____

For "Little Red Riding Hood" a group of fifth graders suggested these titles:

Under Hooded Walks
Tales from Dark Woods
A Girl, a Basket, and a Wolf
Something's Fishy at Grandma's
An Incident of the Innocent Errand

To extend this activity, students can create a matching game using the invented titles and the real ones. Who would guess that "Frosty Apples and Cracked Mirror" went with the beloved story of "Snow White" or "House Construction—A Morality Tale" with "The Three Pigs"?

A final activity for intermediate students is to think of a title for each chapter of a longer novel. I encouraged them to use actual words or phrases from the chapter, as many titles do. For William Sleator's young adult novel *Into the Dream*, students suggested:

Chapter One: "Glowing Object Floating"
Chapter Seven: "Immobilized with Fear"
Chapter Nine: "Utter Bewilderment"

Stories about topics

Stories that include interesting information about a particular topic—for example, animals, bicycles, or sign language—can lead to an engaging learning activity. Before reading the book or the selection, children write down on a "topic worksheet" what they already know about that topic. After they finish reading they add the new information they have learned by reading the story. See Figure 3–17 for a sample of the topic worksheet.

To illustrate, before reading Jean Craighead George's *The Wounded Wolf*, children wrote down what they knew about wolves.

• They aren't really mean.
• They are about size of a dog.
• They live in groups.
• They live in Alaska.

After they had read the story, they recorded what they had learned:

• A group of wolves is called a "pack."
• They can signal to each other with their tails.

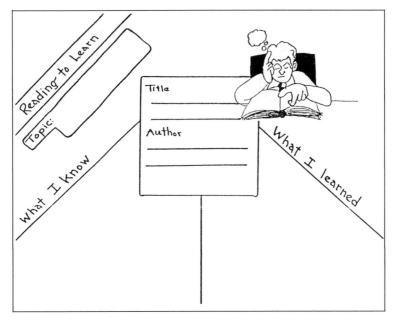

Figure 3–17 Reading-to-Learn Sheet

- They have a very good sense of smell.
- They talk to each other with their barks.
- When one wolf puts his mouth around another's nose, he is saying he is the leader.

Occasionally, the learning center might contain a collection of information about a topic for students to look over *before* they read or listen to a story. One learning center included the title story from Rosebud Yellow Robe's collection of Lakota Indian tales, *Tonweya and the Eagles,* as well as pictures of eagles, short articles about eagles, and an art cutout project relating to eagles. The students learned as much as they could before they read the story. Supplementary information about authors and historical settings, teamed with related stories, can be equally effective.

Sensory writing search

An activity I have used in conjunction with craft lessons (see Chapter 4) is the *sensory writing search.* The object of the activity is to have pairs of students go through a selected story with a fine-tooth comb to find examples of sensory writing, words or phrases the author used that appeal to a reader's sense of sight, hearing, touch, smell, or taste. *Zlateh the Goat,* a story by Isaac Bashevis Singer, one of my favorite writers, proved to be a gold mine of sensory words and phrases. Here are some examples of the words students found, listed according to the five senses:

Looks	*Sounds*	*Feels to touch*	*Smells*	*Tastes*
whirled	whistled	licked her	to fry	was rich
dark as dusk	howled	hand	pancakes	and
cocked her	barked	legs sank		sweet
ears and	bleating	deeper		
listened	began	hands were		
trees covered	to sound	numb		
with	like crying	he choked		
blossoms	wind wailed	when he		
clear brooks	ringing of	breathed		
scratch her	sleigh bells	nose felt		
neck with		like wood		
a horn				
stroke her				
white—				
bearded				
head				

Secret questions

In *The Art of Teaching Writing* Lucy McCormick Calkins introduces an idea that makes a good learning center activity, *secret questions.* (Calkins 1986, 249–252). Using this idea, teachers give students a weekly story and a secret question written on a folded piece of paper to go with that story. Students pair up to discuss their question and try to answer it. (Sometimes they can be encouraged to think of their own secret questions about stories from their folders.) The following are examples of secret questions and the stories I've used them with:

STORY	SECRET QUESTIONS
How the Camel Got Its Hump Rudyard Kipling	Pick one of the author's characters. How well did the author develop this character? Select passages from the story (or see if you can remember) in which

the author showed you how his character looked, spoke, acted, thought and felt, or changed.

I'm in Charge of Celebrations Byrd Baylor	Why do you suppose the author started the story how and where she did? What would be a different way to start the story? Which way do you think would be better?
The White Marble Charlotte Zolotow	What was the setting? Be specific. Where did you first begin to learn about it? How did the author convey the information about the setting? If the story had taken place in a different setting, how would the plot have been similar or different?
Peter's Chair Ezra Jack Keats	What questions would you ask if the author were here? Which would be the most important question? How might the author answer it?
Euphonia and the Flood Mary Calhoun	What do you think of the author's style? If you were in a writing conference with the author, what comments would you make? If you had written the story, what changes would you consider?
Everyone Knows What a Dragon Looks Like Jay Williams	Select (or see if you can remember) a segment in which you think the author has done a particularly good job with description. What makes these sections effective? Be specific. Find words and phrases that carry the description.
Sylvester and the Magic Pebble William Steig	What do you think of the illustrator's style? Why do you suppose he used the medium he used? Was it effective for the purpose? What other styles or media might have been used instead?

Critiques

A final learning center idea that can be used throughout the year focuses on the evaluation of books. As children complete their reading of a book, they file a *critique*. These papers are kept in the classroom in alphabetical order by book title for other students to look through. When a student reads a critique that arouses interest in a story, he or she can request a *reviewer's conference*, in which the interested student and the critic sit and discuss the book. Students may organize their critiques in any way they wish, but they must include some of the following information:

- title
- author
- illustrator
- genre
- publisher
- number of pages
- awards received
- strengths
- weaknesses
- reviewer's comments

Story learning centers offer endless possibilities. Teachers who rely on learning centers develop a management and monitoring system for their use to ensure that the centers become nondisruptive additions to their classrooms. Meaningful learning centers replace workbook pages and skill sheets with a wide range of reading materials and appropriate activities that students can select themselves. In addition, they provide an array of different methods of learning, allow students to practice different reading and writing strategies, and cater to individual learning styles and sensory modes.

FOUR

WRITING
STORIES

As I travel to schools to tell stories and give workshops, it is apparent to me that students' writing is commanding higher visibility in the elementary and middle school curriculum. School hallways are covered with students' illustrated stories, a testament to authorship. Many classrooms proudly display well-organized publishing centers. Often when I perform I share the spotlight with a group of student writers who have won a local young authors' contest, and more times than not, when I leave my suitcase contains a thick, professionally typeset and bound anthology of students' writings as a gift from a school where I have spoken. Teachers today are devising many ingenious ways of stimulating in their student writers a sense of pride and ownership and a feeling of kinship with the world of professional writers. In my school visits I have observed a number of inspiring practices:

- Student writers are given the opportunity to share what they have written or illustrated with other classes in their school building.
- Students are involved in peer-conferencing and critiquing of each other's work in the classroom.
- The books students write have a blank page for comments from fellow writers and teachers.
- Some teachers spend part of their summer at writing conferences, where they produce stories and poems to bring back to the classroom and share with their students.
- Students attend special statewide conferences where they read their work to other students and elicit their responses.

- Some students' work is professionally bound and sold nationally as trade books to libraries and schools.
- Students are writing letters to the authors they are reading. With the insight of a fellow practitioner, they are asking astute questions about the writing craft.
- Many schools allot funds each year to invite a published author to visit and speak with the student body.
- Some schools conduct preplanned telephone interviews with the students' favorite authors.

Books on the "writing process" approach are widely available. Lucy McCormick Calkins, Donald Graves, Jane Hansen, Nancie Atwell, and Donald Murray are just a few of the writer-researchers who are reinvigorating and redirecting classroom writing strategies. Terms such as *process, conferencing, mini-lessons, writing logs,* and *writer's workshop* are quickly becoming mainstream educational jargon. In this chapter I will focus on some of the techniques I have used in writing stories—most of them with intermediate-aged students, students in or around third grade who have reached a level of proficiency in their reading and writing skills that allows them to become immersed in the actual craft of story writing. They have moved from exclusively expository writing to writing that has the shape and feel of narrative. No longer are their renderings simply recountings of personal events or the fanciful forays of their wild imaginations. They are instead deliberate efforts to structure events (real or imagined) according to the format of a story. With varying degrees of success, their stories begin to show signs of a beginning, middle, and end. They begin to see titles as significant, and use dialogue to reveal character rather than fill space ("Hello, how are you?" she asked. "Fine, how are you?" he said). They describe settings skillfully and selectively, and portray problems or conflicts effectively. Along the way, these older students are gaining more confidence in the mechanics of writing—the conventions of spelling, punctuation, and sentence structure. They are also experimenting with literary devices such as metaphor and personification. They are developing an ear sensitive to the sound values of language—to alliteration and word play.

A MODEL OF THE WRITING PROCESS

Writing process may in the end prove to be a great misnomer. Not only is *process* redundant, since writing is by its very nature a process, but labeling it as such implies that there is one universal, linear, step-by-step procedure that all writers (beginning or professional) go through in writing. The term *writing process* seems at times to suggest the directions for building a model airplane: step 1, step 2 . . . finished product. In reality, each writer has highly personal working methods, whether conscious or unconscious. Each time a writer begins to write, a unique variation of this personal process occurs. It is an oversimplification to assume that if we teach writing as a step-by-step process, our students will automatically become efficient writers.

Having said that, I would now like to argue that most writers use the skeleton of a "writing process" to varying degrees at various times in their writing and that this sequence can be presented, taught, and used in a classroom setting. By involving themselves in the actual practices writers use, children begin to discover their own personal routes to successful writing. Each time writers practice their craft, they discover more about what works for them. As I tell my students, we do not necessarily get better at writing itself, but we do get better at recognizing when we are not functioning at *our* best in our writing.

In my classroom, I explained the writing process model in terms of *fingering, styling, eye-balling,* and *copying.*

It is important to point out immediately that, although the illustration shows the process model as a linear, left-to-right procedure, this may not describe the actual process writers go through. Writers often move back and forth between the steps in a recursive fashion. When I start a story and am "fingering" or exploring story ideas on paper, I may use a jot list or free-writing exercise. Later, when I am involved in drafting sentences about those ideas ("styling"), I may need to turn to another fingering activity if I discover that I need more information. When I am editing ("eye-balling"), I may swing back and forth between styling and editing if I determine that what I have written sounds flat or redundant. Often, it is not until I think I am happy with a story and am copying it as a final draft that I discover some overlooked editing concern. I then must return to that stage. Like a stream with many eddies, the writing process must at times curl back upon itself to maintain its consistent flow.

FINGERING

The *fingering* stage of the writing process is nothing more than a way of beginning, of gathering and formulating ideas. It is the time for choosing the direction of a piece and working it out, to a degree, before the first draft. Fingering activities come in many shapes, from scribbled notes and lists to formal outlines, from four or five experimental lead paragraphs to a sure-fire collection of possible titles. These activities can best be described as "backstage work." I have chosen the term "fingering" because it suggests the use of a pencil and the keyboard of a word processor. Using a pencil or a word processor, students begin the work of putting their thoughts on paper.

In story writing, the fingering stage enables writers to gather ideas, structure a story's design, and generate information for a story. I have already described two activities that fall in the fingering stage. Both the story triggering sheet and the story sequence sheet (see page 60) help writers organize and plan their ideas for a story. In addition, the triggering sheet also helps generate specific sensory details for possible use in a story.

Before they worry about organization, however, students need story ideas. Professional writers get their ideas in many ways and from many directions. Clyde Robert Bulla says he looks into life:

> Ask yourself what interests you, what you fear, love, or hate. Write down your answers. See if they don't suggest stories. Ideas are everywhere. The thing is to reorganize them and learn how to use them.

And children's writer Julia Cunningham echoes him:

> To me ideas arrive from anywhere—overheard conversations, a glance from a stranger, a sprained ankle, etc., etc., but, most certainly from emotional experiences—grief, the necessity for survival, the cause of sudden laughter—whatever changes or uplifts or affects.

I have my own potential story ideas jotted down in a small notebook I keep at my desk. My father's fastidious refinishing of an ornate old coffee table when I was a boy still heads the list as something I want to develop into a story someday. There's also an entry about my stepson's humorous encounter with a junior high teacher. Under that is written "Rhyme: What to do when you are stuck, stuck, s . . . t . . . u . . . c . . . k," where I've noted that I want to write a rhyme or jingle to use in my classes when a student says he is "stuck." To help them watch for their own possible story ideas and hold on to them when they occurred, each of my beginning writers had a writing folder. Stapled to the opening page was an ongoing writing inventory divided into three categories: wonderings, story ideas, and things I know a lot about (see Figure 4–1). During the writing workshop if children finished a writing project they might refer back to the inventory to see if one of their ideas might be ready to be developed into a story.

To reinforce for my students the idea of holding on to story ideas, of writing them down in their folders, I've always read them Arnold Lobel's wonderful tale from *Frog and Toad Are Friends* called "The Story." In the story, Frog isn't feeling well and Toad is looking after him. Bedridden Frog requests a story from Toad, but, try as he may, Toad cannot think of one. First, he tries walking up and down the porch. That doesn't help. Then he stands on his head. No story comes. He pours water on his head and bangs his head on the wall. Still no story comes. Finally, exhausted, without a story, and not feeling so well, Toad crawls into bed and asks if Frog might tell him a story. Frog is more than happy to and proceeds to tell the

Figure 4–1 Writing Folder Sheet

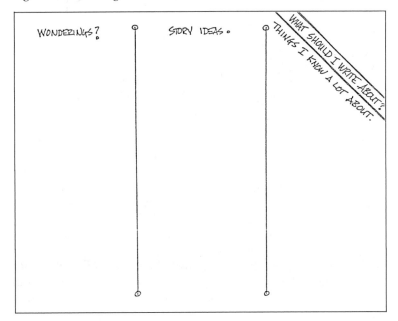

Figure 4–2 "Story Idea Search" Sheet

story of a toad and the different things he did trying to think up a story for his friend Frog. "Unlike Toad," I told my classes, "you'll not need to drench yourselves and bang your heads trying to find story ideas. Your writing folders will always have another idea for you to experiment with."

From time to time I assigned children a *story idea search*, in which they were to gather from all around them (not only at school but throughout their day-to-day lives) interesting possibilities for stories. The collected these together on a sheet they also kept in their folders (see Figure 4–2). I encouraged them to be on the lookout for:

- "Hmm's and wonderings"—ideas and things they wondered about.
- "Caught my attention"—things they paused to look at.
- "Now that's interesting"—quirky, interesting, day-to-day events and happenings.
- "Noticings and word snapshots"—things they noticed that they would have taken a picture of if they could.

One of the ways children might start developing a story from these story ideas is through the technique of *brainstorming*. In brainstorming students unleash all the information they have about a topic before beginning to write anything. Typically, when students brainstorm, they write down as quickly as possible everything that pops into their heads about an idea. Correct spelling and proper penmanship are annoying barriers to effective brainstorming. I have told my students to let the gates fly open: "Don't think and analyze— WRITE. And WRITE as quickly as you can."

Taking a story idea about her big sister, one youngster began brainstorming, using a jot list:

sometimes friend of mine
sometimes cruel to me
taught me how to sew
sometimes babysits me and won't talk to me
has frosted hair
once ate cigarette butts out of an ashtray as a baby
goes to the mall a lot with her friends
good ice skater
doesn't come home until very late sometimes

The list then became the foundation for her thinking about her story. By going over her entries she decided first if a story was possible, then what information would be relevant, what wouldn't, what could be developed, what needed to be discarded, and what other alleys she might need to explore. A brainstormed list can also lead the writer to see a pattern not otherwise obvious. This youngster might discover that big sisters can be sweet and sour—they can be buddies at one time and cruel older sisters at another. That very emotional pendulum might become the focus of a story about the ups and downs of little-big sister relationships, a much larger story than a mere recounting of an older sister's characteristics.

In a similar vein, my students would take a clean sheet of unlined white paper, write a story idea in the middle of it, and then brainstorm. To dig for a possible plot behind the idea, they used what we called *story sketching questions.* They jotted answers to these questions at random in the blank areas around the story idea:

- What happened? Why? What were the consequences?
- What could happen then? What else?
- Why would a character think that way?
- How would he react?
- What would happen as a result of that reaction?
- What would happen after that?
- How might a different character think? React?
- What are the possible results of two different characters thinking and reacting differently?
- What would these characters end up doing?
- What would happen then?

Struggling over possible answers to these questions would often help direct their story ideas into stories with plots.

An interim practice before drafting is to have the students take another clean sheet of paper and divide it into three equal parts—beginning, middle, and end. After they cross out the things on the brainstorming list they don't think they want to include in the story, they categorize what is left by putting it in one of the three sections. This technique helps them focus the direction of their narrative: Is it going to follow a chronological pattern? Will they try a flashback? What kind of lead would be effective in foreshadowing something appearing later in the story?

Some writers employ a technique called a "free-write" in which they simply start writing about a topic or story idea as quickly and unconsciously as they can. The purpose of a free-write is to unclog the pathway from the brain to the paper. In this process, writers try for a serendipitous flow in their words: it forces the mind to get working and the words to keep coming. Often a free-write acts like the unplugging of a hole in a dike—a drip at first but soon a torrent of words, often more than the writer's pencil can handle. I encouraged my students to try a free-write only after they had organized their ideas in some fashion (a story triggering sheet, a story sequence sheet, a jot list, or brainstorming with story sketching questions). Since a free-write often became the basis of a first draft, I wanted them to have at least some initial plan that would carry them through once the free-write got them started.

Fingering activities force students to think out their plans for their stories (even if they don't necessarily stick to the original ideas) and allow them to get down on paper something they can use as an in-process reference. Often, children have great ideas for stories and want to start writing immediately. But, when their initial burst of creativity wanes, if they have done no planning or recording of their thoughts, they have nothing to fall back on. They can only terminate the story or revert to the "action-reaction" mode. In essence, they have started putting up walls without a supporting scaffolding. The results can be frustrating at best, at worst, disastrous.

STYLING

Styling, as I use it, is best defined as "earfully attentive drafting." It is writing in which preferential concern is given to how a piece "sounds." The story's creator is beginning to record words, sentences, descriptions, and dialogue that he or she wants readers to "hear" as they read. If the fingering stage is the place for gathering, planning, and thinking, the styling stage is where the writer begins to shape those ideas into a working draft. In the illustration of the writing process in my classroom (p. 111), the styling stage is represented by an ear. I explain to students that the "ear" is a writer's greatest friend and ally. It acts as confidant, sounding board, and unseen audience. "Every writer," I said, "needs a comfortable working relationship with his or her ear."

To a degree, the styling stage resembles the early writing efforts of very young children when they talk to themselves as they write, reading aloud what they believe they have written. They may try to show the expression they hear in their speaking voices by capitalizing important words, underlining groups of words, or writing certain words larger or darker. In the same way, I encourage student writers to read their drafts aloud as they write. "How does it sound? Do your written words capture the flow and expression of the words you hear in your head?" I ask them. As I write, I constantly go back over what I have written, reading it aloud and trying to imagine what a reader would be hearing. Judging it from that perspective, I may go back and change a word, add some information, or redraft a sentence in order to achieve the desired flow.

Students' writing often has only a faint correspondence to the "sound" of the stories they really want to tell. Their writing seems a "cheap imitation" of the natural, expressive way they talk. In the transition from speech to print, the colorful, rhythmic quality of spoken language is lost to "words-on-paper prose": No cadence, no flow, and—worst of all—no surprises! Although student writers speak freely and fluently, they are frustrated when they have to capture their words on paper. I have sometimes accused my students of writing sentences that sound like workbook exercises:

> Once there was a man. He was a good man. He did many good things. One day . . .

"How would you tell that story aloud?" I ask them. "How can you create on paper an interesting way for readers to hear the story as if they were listening to you tell it?"

> A good man there was once, known far and wide for his goodly deeds—deeds of compassion, deeds of a selfless fashion. One day . . .

Now *that* is beginning to sound like a story. During the styling stage, I always remind children to trust their ears, to rely on what they hear. In Strunk and White's classic text on writing, *The Elements of Style,* White speaks clearly and succinctly about the "sound" of written language: "Who can confidently say," he asks, "what ignites a certain combination of words, causing them to explode in the mind?" The answer lies in part in the "sound words make on paper" (Strunk and White 1959,66). "Listen to what you write," he advises.

To encourage children to listen to the sound of their stories, I called on the storytelling stool. During the writing workshop, students could take a draft of what they were working on and give it (or a part of it) a "sound check" by reading the draft from the stool. Listening students would fill out a *story styling check sheet.* Across the top of the sheet was a set of numbers for rating how the story sounded. Each student would give the story a score and write comments in the space below (see Figure 4–3). Along with the story styling check, students would consider each other's stories in terms of what we called "styling questions":

- Does the voice in the piece sound like the author's?
- Does it show evidence of carefully chosen, interesting words and unusual ways of saying things?
- Does it allow readers or listeners to see in their minds exactly what the writer is describing?
- Are there sensory details?
- Is any information left out?
- Are there any places where information might have been better left out?

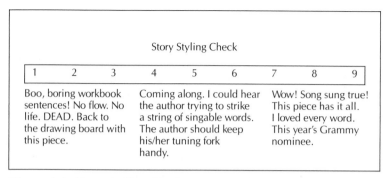

Figure 4–3 Story Styling Check

- Does the dialogue give the effect of real characters talking?
- Are there any confusing parts?
- Does the lead draw readers or listeners into the story?
- Is the conclusion persuasive?
- Are the sentences effective? Too bulky or too choppy?

Another effective approach used by many teachers has been referred to as *sentence lifting*. The teacher takes individual sentences from a student's story and the class experiments with redrafting them. Following one of my own classroom maxims—*There is always more than one way to put words into a sentence*—my students would explore the various ways individual sentences could be redesigned. For example:

Lionel the lion is a party animal. He likes music, dancing, and singing.

might be redrafted as:

Lionel the lion is one music-mad, paw-pawing, sing-singing forest animal. Lionel's his name, but partying's his game. The forest swings to his lion's beat.

Together, we discovered that more effective writing surprises us with its word arrangement. We learned that the realignment of a clause aids the flow of a sentence and that breaking the repetitive pattern of sentences holds the attention of the reader. As the *Wanted Poster* in the writing workshop stated, good style comes from good word choice:

WANTED

To be used in our writing

Tasteful,
tuneful,
ear-tingling words.
Right words
tight words
utter-delight words.

EYEBALLING

Lively writing involves both play and work. During the styling stage of story writing, children approached their task with a playful attitude. They wrote quickly and flippantly, sensing that too much deliberation over spelling or punctuation can interrupt the narrative flow. They were concerned about whether they could get all their incoming thoughts written down, and how those thoughts sounded. They decided whether information was appropriate and whether they were catching the reader's attention with "tasteful, tuneful, ear tingling words." The editing or *eyeballing* stage however, was truly work. Students had to slow down, rein in their natural tendency to want to be done, look at their piece, and remember all the mind-boggling details of written language. They had to think about proper spelling, placement of apostrophes, and appropriate marks of punctuation—all the conventions of standard grammar.

As I explained, the eye is the writer's objectifier. It allows a necessary distance from a piece of writing. Through the eye, writers become their own second reader and editor. "We need to train our eyes," I told them, "to spot errors we typically make during the frenzied styling of our drafts. We ought to view our eyes as invisible friends that will help us in getting our truest writing voices onto paper." In the classroom we kept an oversized pair of glasses to represent the idea that when we edited we wore "glasses" that brought our full attention to our work and to our mistakes in the mechanics of writing.

Our classroom had an Eyeballing Station fully equipped with red pencils, dictionaries, punctuation guides, a thesaurus, and a list of simplified grammar rules. The expectation at this station was simple—students were to edit conscientiously, but only to their level of competency. Students were not to worry about making each and every manuscript letter-perfect. "Correctness is an attitude," I told them, "a desire on the part of the writer to make a piece as correct as he or she can."

As an editing reminder, students kept an *eyeballing checklist* in their writing folders with overall questions such as these:

- Have I checked any questionable spellings in my piece?
- Have I read and reread for missing or left-out words?
- Have I worked with any parts that have been pointed out as confusing or misleading?
- Have I used nouns and verbs instead of an overabundance of adjectives and adverbs?
- Have I examined my sentences? Are they complete? Too long? Too repetitive? Too short?

The checklist also listed particular points of grammar, which we called the *nit-picks:*

NIT-PICKS—HAVE I CHECKED?

- quotation marks
- commas
- sentences:
    complete
    varied
    punctuated correctly
- verb tenses
- splitting words at ends of lines
- paragraphing:
    useful to reader
    indented
- odd punctuation:
    apostrophes
    ellipses
    colons
    contractions
    single quotations

In addition to these nit-picking errors, my students were also familiar with *Mr. Denman's Pen Sins* (and at times were required to chorus these in strict, straight-faced cadence):

- Never under any circumstances bore me with generalities—include details, examples, and/or specifics.
- Don't hide behind your words. I want to know that a person—a real, live, breathing, dreaming, caring person—wrote the story.

- Use vague, boring, and overused verbs only at your own risk—try lively, "to-the-point" verbs to catch my attention.
- Vary, vary, vary—experiment with sentence length, sentence structure, and paragraph lengths.

If the purpose of the styling stage is to give a piece the feel of a "told" story, then that of the eyeballing stage is to construct prose for "sound," to offer to the readers' eyes exactly what the writer wants them to hear. Unfortunately, there is no direct, one-to-one correspondence between spoken language and printed language. What students put on paper is often only a shadow of what they hear in their own heads and want to say. Spoken language has at its command pauses, changes in intonation, and volume, not to mention facial expression—all of which add to its effectiveness. Like landscape painting, written prose can only give an impression of the story being told. We do not see every detail of the setting or the subtle movements of the character. The reader constructs meaning from the brushstrokes on the page. This aspect of writing may be one of the most challenging obstacles young writers face.

I encouraged children to take a draft to a quiet corner, cover their ears with their hands, and imagine they were reading it for the very first time. "What would the reader be hearing?" I asked them. "Is it the same thing you, the writer, want them to hear? How would you construct your words so that the reader and the writer hear just about the same thing?" Using the sentence lifting technique once again, we would take a paragraph, project it onto the board, and, together discuss how it could be redrafted to better serve the reader. Along the way we would correct the "nit-picks": "Who can tell me which form of 'to' we would use here? This verb is rather drab—let's brainstorm for some options. Did the writer keep the proper tense here?"

Another technique I found useful was my *O.O.P.S.ing* sheets. The acronym was conceived by a writing committee and used throughout the district where I taught. It stood for *Often Overlooked Proofreading Skills*. My O.O.P.S.ing sheet was simply a list of ten or fifteen common nit-picking mistakes I found in students' drafts or stories. When I read through their folders, I would write down any common mistakes. Then I would run these off on a transparency, and we would discuss and correct them as a class. Figure 4–4 shows one week's example.

By using O.O.P.S.ing sheets, students reviewed and corrected the common mistakes that plagued their work. Rather than taking the time to teach one full lesson with practice sheets and test questions on, for example, *there, their,* and *they're,* I would simply include the three variations on the weekly O.O.P.S.ing sheets. If, in going over their drafts, I found that many of the students were making the same mistakes, I would review that particular skill with the whole class.

Another technique I employed from time to time was to assemble *student grammar committees,* each responsible for one skill. Drafts of individual stories would pass through the hands of these small groups of students. Working together, one group would consider the paper's sentence structure, another its proper or improper use of capitalization. At the end of the month, each group would present a *state of the grammar* address to the class on how well we were

Figure 4–4 "O.O.P.S.ing" Sheet

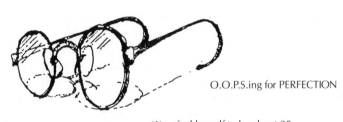

O.O.P.S.ing for PERFECTION

(1) ...feel herself to be about 25

(2) ecpecialy

(3) ...and where glasses

(4) wrenkled

(5) renber

(6) intil

(7) My Grandmother...

(8) &

(9) ...she's was in 4th grade

(10 knever

(11) ...That really care's for you

(12) She was ten year's old she's nice, pretty,
and good grades and she is funny

(13) ...wierd...

(14) ...strang...

(15 ...to many skins

using their skill. They were also responsible for creating and conducting a craft lesson on their skill. In a similar way, a group of students was occasionally selected to serve as *eyeball editors*. Working from the Eyeball Station, they were responsible for helping other students with any editing questions.

In the end, what I attempted to create in my classroom was the feeling that no one is a perfect writer—that the mistakes that occur in students' writing are the mistakes that all writers make. At times, I would even bring in one of my own story drafts, complete with its omissions and misspellings. I wanted children to adopt the attitude that, when they work hard at writing a story, part of their job is to apply what they know of the conventions of written language. And I wanted them to be confident that what they needed to know about grammar and the mechanics of writing would come in good time. They only had to keep writing.

COPYING

When all the other stages are completed, the writer carefully makes a final draft for the writing folder, the computer diskette, or a bound and illustrated display book. At first glance, the *copying* stage may seem the easiest and the most self-evident. The real trick to copying, however, is not the act of copying itself but the decision about when a draft is ready to be copied. In my own writing, I am never sure when I have revised and edited a piece enough. Children often want to copy too soon, before they have reworked their stories enough to achieve any authentic voice. Or they are so anxious not to make any mistakes in the final version they whittle the original story idea down to what I call "safe mush"—no flow, no surprise, no story.

There is a point in the process at which the story and the writer beg for things to be brought to closure. When students would ask me if I thought their stories were ready to be copied, I usually responded with two questions: Have you learned enough from this story? and Are you happy with it? Affirmative answers to both those questions suggested that it was probably time for the piece to be published in some form so the writer could move on to other projects. Unlike a graduate school thesis that "begs" to be finished so we *never* have to write another one, a story needs to be finished to make way for the next story struggling to be heard. Stories beget more stories. One satisfaction of finishing a story about my grandfather was that, in the process, my grandmother's story came to life.

My intermediate students used a list of *"author consideration topics"* to help them think about whether or not a story was ready to be copied and finished. Although the list contains eleven topics, I explained that they need only spend time with two: one they chose and one I chose. Taking their drafts, they would consider these two topics (use of detail and dialogue, for example) and give their work a final think-through and revision if needed. "Think like an author," I advised them. Here is the list:

AUTHOR CONSIDERATION TOPICS

1. *Examples.* Have I used them to illustrate what I am talking about?
2. *Details.* Did I include enough so my reader can "see" my story?
3. *Dialogue.* Did I create the "feel" of real characters talking?
4. *Revision.* Did I stay with the point of the story? Do I need to cut parts? Add parts?
5. *Lead.* Did I attempt to capture my reader's attention?
6. *Closing.* Did I bring the story to a close? Any loose ends?
7. *Title.* Would I want to read a story with this title?
8. *Sequence.* Does the story follow a logical, readable order?
9. *Suspense.* Did I use cliffhangers or other techniques to keep the reader involved?
10. *Point of view.* Did I think through and use a consistent point of view?
11. *Stylistics.* Were my word choices and phrasing fresh and pleasant to the ear?

Children kept records of their writing endeavors on a sheet stapled to the last page of their writing folders (see Figure 4–5). Here they recorded the titles of their stories, when they completed the first draft, if they had a group critique either through a styling sound check or a grammar committee, if they had conferences (or author talks); and finally when and how the stories were published.

A final aspect of the copying stage is determining if and how to evaluate the final result. Marking, grading, and evaluating students' efforts present an incessantly thorny issue—no matter how we hold it, it still pricks us. We are all familiar with the general concern about marking written papers:

• Do students necessarily "learn" from their teacher-marked papers? How many times have they been glanced at quickly and thrown away?

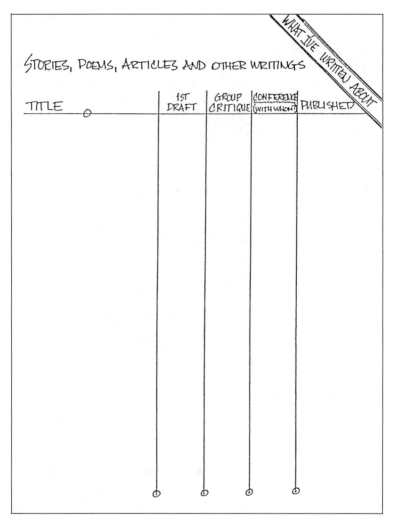

Figure 4–5 Writing Folder Sheet

- Does marking up a paper eventually turn kids off to writing?
- Could the time invested in grading be better spent in other, more productive areas? In more extensive planning, perhaps?
- Finally, does the need for time-consuming grading tend to steer teachers away from involving students with writing assignments

and toward easily graded multiple-choice worksheets?

The same concerns hold true for story writing. Should we even be grading stories written by young writers? Having taught incoming education students on the college level for a few years now, I feel negligent if I don't stress the fact that education is a graded endeavor. Students are graded, teachers are graded, principals are graded, superintendents are graded, and school boards are graded. As much as teachers would love to have their children simply learn without the need for this kind of comparison, the educational system as it now stands, is predicated on just such an approach. How individual teachers handle this in their classrooms in view of the mandates and demands of their school districts will always be an individual challenge.

In my classroom I used several approaches to evaluation that seemed to work. First, of course, the students kept writing folders containing a record of their individual output, which could serve as the basis for a grade. To this I added a self-evaluation system through the use of a *writer's checklist* (see Figure 4–6). When students finished a story, they would evaluate themselves by circling numbers along a rating scale. By comparing this checklist with their evaluations of earlier work, students could see if they were improving.

I also had children fill out *personal reminder pencils* to keep in their writing folders. These were narrow strips of tagboard cut in the shape of a pencil. On one side it said: THE NEXT TIME I WRITE A STORY I'LL BE THINKING ABOUT. . . . On the other side was a blank space. When they finished a story, the students were to think of and write down one idea about story writing they needed or wanted to remember for their next story. For example, one student wrote "How will I get my readers interested in my story when they read my first lines?" and another, "Will my setting fit my story? Can I use colorful words when I describe it?" The children completed personal reminder pencils for each successive story and kept them in their folders as personal reminders throughout the year. In the writing workshop I encouraged them to pull out and review their pencils before starting a new story.

The personal reminder pencils helped children focus on their own writing concerns and generate, over time, much more specific thoughts about their writing. So often in recent years when students talk about their writing during my school visits, their comments are so vague and generic that they couldn't possibly be helpful. They

Writer's Checklist
Self-Evaluation

How Are You Doing?

1	2	3	4	5	6	7	8	9

Honest Writing
Yuck. Who am I fooling? I've got words in my head – I should use them!

I can hear myself. It's beginning to sound like me as a writer.

Marvelous! Reads like me talking to the reader.

1	2	3	4	5	6	7	8	9

Details
What is this? I can't see a thing I've described. Vague.

I'll keep adding specifics. They make writing "seeable."

I can see it! Concrete details, vivid descriptions. I was there. So will the reader be there.

1	2	3	4	5	6	7	8	9

Verbs
Dead flies! Boo! Call the surgeon!

Better... I've got to look at more of my verbs. I can find even better words.

This writing has bounce. Super-stupendous verbology! I'm proud.

1	2	3	4	5	6	7	8	9

Capitals and End Punctuation
Quick to the doctor! I need my eyeballs checked!

Still need closer examination. I need to find the boundaries of EACH sentence.

Perfect! I'll hire out as a copy editor.

1	2	3	4	5	6	7	8	9

Punctuation and Spelling
I'm in trouble. I should never be out of arm's reach of a dictionary.

A couple errors – I think I could have found them myself if I'd taken a closer look.

Wonderful! I've got one finely tuned eyeball.

1	2	3	4	5	6	7	8	9

Word Play
Hey, what's the matter with me? Ain't I got any word-imagination?

I'm coming along. I should take more risks. Try some strange words in weird places. Trust my ear.

Love it. "Oh, what a clever wordologist I am!"

Figure 4–6 Writer's Checklist for Self-Evaluation

say, "I need to be creative when I write" or "I need to use my imagination more." I insisted that my students write specific, to-the-point reminders: not "The next time I write a story I will be thinking about characters" but "The next time I write a story I will be thinking about developing my characters so my readers can truly see them in their minds."

Here is what a group of fourth and fifth graders wrote on their personal reminder pencils after a series of writing workshops.

THE NEXT TIME I WRITE A STORY I'LL BE THINKING ABOUT...

- Using a "grabby" title that catches the reader's attention.
- Will I want a happy or sad ending?
- What could I include in my story that makes my reader's blood pump?
- Will I want to write a second story to tell more of my character's adventures?
- Will my story be well-worded with correct information?
- Will my conclusion wrap up my story and finish my story well?
- Will my lead entice the reader into continuing my story?
- Does my ending alert the reader that the story has ended?
- Giving my characters names that fit them.
- Writing so the reader is "in" the story, enjoying and understanding it.
- Making sure the whole story fits like a puzzle.
- Letting my readers know how my characters act and feel.
- Using more suspense that keeps the reader anxious about what's going to happen next.
- Not using a lot of violence in Greg Denman's Writing Workshop.
- Sketching out my story ideas before writing my story.
- Mixing up the feelings of my story: happy, sad, funny, strange.
- Making sure my story is interesting enough to satisfy the reader.
- Letting the characters form in my mind so that they will seem real.
- Writing a conclusion that makes the reader go "Ahhh."
- Having extra ideas in case one doesn't work out.

In addition to the self-evaluation scores and the personal reminder pencils, I could assign actual letter grades to stories. When I did, I used double grades, one for mechanics and the other for writing style. In my classroom, children would receive what we called an "eyeballing" grade and an "earing" grade. The criteria sheet for this system looks something like this:

EYEBALLING GRADE	EARING GRADE
O.O.P.S.ing	**Earing**

Has the writer checked:
    questionable spellings?
    endmarks?
    capitals?
    other punctuation?
    contractions?
    homonyms?
    complete sentences?
    legibility?

Does it sound as if the writer is talking?
Does it make sense?
Is it vivid?
Does it have strong, fresh verbs?
Does it have some:
    surprising words?
    enjoyable wordings?

To complement these two grades I wrote out evaluative comments, often in the form of short personal letters, on the final drafts of many of the students' stories. While grades and self-evaluation scores may draw children's attention to aspects of their writing, a personal response stays with them because it indicates that someone has bothered to take their writing seriously. My written evaluations were based on the following questions:

- What has the writer attempted? What has the writer achieved?
- Is there an honest, personal feel to the writing? Does it sound like that student's voice? Vocabulary?
- Has the student attempted to use words effectively? Verbs (stronger, more vivid)? Descriptors (more appropriate, concrete)?
- Is there evidence of word play? Of connotative rather than just denotative use of words? Puns? Clever wordings?
- Is there evidence of a plan or guiding organization in the writing? Is it logical? Thought-out?
- If dialogue is used, is the use of quotations effective? Is the language appropriate to the speaker? Are the characters believable? Does the reader have the opportunity to come to know them?
- Is the language vivid? Are things described in detail? Is there evidence that the writer is striving to have us "see-in-our-minds" what he is writing about?
- Is the proofreading strong or weak? Is it careless or are the mistakes due to an attempt to use more complex sentence structure? Do mistakes appear in areas the student should be familiar with? Is this paper showing progress or regression in writing mechanics?

Throughout the evaluation process I try to remember John Masefield's timeless words: "Great writing evolves more from great encouragement than from great criticism."

AUTHOR TALKS

Today, many writing researchers and teachers refer to the technique of "conferencing," in which students react—with others—to their own writing. Conferences offer a way to iron out the specific problems young writers are experiencing with a text. Most often they are oral discussions of a draft and can be held with the teacher or with peers. In my classroom we called conferences *author talks.* These were similar to conferences but limited in scope and provided a more personal way of doing things. In essence, they were discussions between practicing writers.

Billy: "Mr. D., I'd like to find time for an author talk."

Mr. D.: "Fine, Billy, would love to. Please make sure you've thought out what we can talk about."

(Later)

Mr. D.: "How's it going, Billy?"

Billy: "So-so."

Mr. D.: "So, what would you like to talk about?"

Billy: "I'm having problems with my story."

Mr. D.: "OK, you're the writer. Tell me about it."

Billy: "I don't know how to finish it."

Mr. D.: "So, how would an author talk about that problem?"

Billy: "Hmm . . . I'm having problems with the conclusion."

Mr. D.: "Sounds good enough for a start. What kinds of things should an author be thinking about in regard to conclusions?"

Billy: "The loose ends of his story tied up . . ."

Mr. D.: "Yes, and . . ."

Billy: "Some kind of resolution to the story's problem."

Mr. D.: "Good. So tell me about your story's problem."

Billy: "Well . . . this guy is angry at his friends . . ."

Mr. D.: (*interrupting*) "This guy?"

Billy: "One of the story's main characters is angry at his friends because they won't let him join their secret club."

Mr. D.: "Why not?"

Billy: "They're mean."

Mr. D.: "Just mean—why are they mean? What does an author need to know about why characters act the way they do?"

Billy: "The characters' motivation?"

Mr. D.: "You got it! So what's the motivation of these guys . . . these characters? Why are they mean?"

Billy: "I don't know—I just made them mean."

Mr. D.: "And the guy—why does he want to join their club?"

Billy: "Because it's cool."

Mr. D.:   "Now there's some motivation. People want to be included in the activities of their friends. It's cool to be a part of a group. Your readers will relate to that. So what's the character going to do about this situation?"

Billy: "I'm not sure."

Mr. D.:   "Have you tried brainstorming possible actions he can take?"

Billy: "Not yet."

Mr. D.:   "Well, my suggestion for now is, before you worry about ending the piece, first consider the motivation of his friends. Why are they excluding him? Then, do a jot list of all the possible recourses available to him, with their possible consequences, and see where the story takes you from there. We can talk again later if you'd like."

During the author talk, I attempt at every turn to urge the student to think and talk like a writer. I hoped that, after an ongoing series of such experiences children would begin to adopt the language and thinking processes of writers.

The author talks in my classroom were spontaneous, but I attempted to point students in useful directions:

• To think like an author.

   What would an author think about here? What should a writer consider here? How might an author react here?

• To rehearse the use of story language.

   What do we call that? How would an author refer to that?

• To summarize their writing concerns.

   Let's remember how we said authors reveal their characters. For today, let's think about three possible strategies to use when you are stuck with a story like this . . .

• To consider suggestions.

   Have you tried . . . ?
   Here's an idea . . . ?
   Why don't you . . . ?

I developed a series of ice-breaking questions to help students begin to talk about their stories. Here are a few of them:

- What would you like to talk about?
- What writing concerns do you have?
- Show me your best passage. What makes it good?
- Show me your worst passage. How would a writer go about making it better?
- If you had to choose one (and only one) area you needed to work on with this piece, what would it be?
- What have you learned from this story?
- How will you approach your next story differently?
- Tell me about the fingering process for this story.
- What did you learn from your styling critique?
- How successful were you with your eyeballing?
- Did you have any surprises or discoveries during the writing?
- How would you compare this story to others you've written? Others you've read? Why?
- Where did this story come from? Is it leading you to another?
- What passage best sums up the entire story?
- Tell me how you feel about your lead paragraph?
- Are you happy with your ending?
- What might improve either the lead or the ending?
- Are your characters real? Are you happy with how they appear on paper?
- Does your title work for you? How did you come up with it?

In the final analysis, author talks are what their title implies—one author talking about a story with another. They encourage the beginning writer to role-play using the language and thought processes of writers until these become their own.

CRAFT LESSONS

Different types of writing demand different things of a writer. Stories are clearly not poems, and poems are not editorials. Editorials require a different focus than science reports, and science reports are inherently different from humorous sketches. No matter how experienced students become with the writing process in general, their success with different genres is based on the instruction and the examples they are given. In my classroom, such instruction was called a *craft lesson*.

A craft lesson was a presentation or demonstration, generally to the whole class, in the course of a writing workshop. It could consist of a month-long look at character portrayals or a quick three-minute review of a particularly well-written passage, either by a published author or a student. It could focus on the construction of leads or story plotting, on an author's theme or depiction of setting, or on character motivation or the use of folktale structure. Those who are familiar with the work of Lucy McCormick Calkins (*The Art of Teaching Writing*) and her associates may see similarities between craft lessons and *mini-lessons*. In essence, a craft lesson is simply a lesson or presentation that is designed to draw students' attention to the ways practicing writers go about their writing. In terms of stories, it is an insider's view of the craft. Over the years I have presented craft lessons about:

- *Personal writing:* how authors have used events from their own lives in their stories.
- *Flashback techniques:* how a flashback can be used in a story.
- *Descriptive details:* how authors go about using sensory details effectively, particularly in reference to story settings.
- *Dialogues:* how effective dialogue gives the illusion of spoken language.
- *Folk structures:* how a folktale can be rewritten to reflect different cultures or ethnic groups.
- *Home-rooted language:* how authors handle the spoken vernacular of the characters in a story.
- *Leads:* how authors grab their readers and set the "promise" for their stories.
- *Closings:* how authors bring closure to their stories and how they achieve what they want readers to feel at the end of a story.
- *Titles:* effective and not-so-effective titles for stories, and what makes a title effective.
- *Action:* how stories are held together through the action of the character(s).
- *Genres:* similarities and differences between realistic fiction, science fiction, fantasy, autobiography, folktales, humorous sketches, and suspense stories.

In addition to these practitioner's craft lessons I also focused some craft lessons on the mechanics of writing:

- Sentence combining and sentence variety.
- Correct use of quotation marks with written dialogues.
- Word clutter and word repetition.
- Consistency of voice and verb tense.
- Paragraphing.
- Splitting words at the ends of lines.
- Comma usage.
- Apostrophe usage.

TOOLS FOR LITERARY TOUCHES

Beyond the basics of a well-designed and well-written story lie the fine touches—literary devices. Most writers try to master these devices and to use them aptly and at will. Imagery, metaphor, and the related tools in a writer's toolbox make the difference between the words of Shakespeare and their paraphrase, between an eloquent essay and a brief journal entry, between a good novel and Cliff Notes. Literary devices take full advantage of the richness language has to offer.

Helping children to appreciate literary devices and to use them in their writing is not the work of a day. In my experience, it is mostly highly literate children, the ones who read widely and voraciously, who seem to use literary devices in their writing naturally. The majority of children, like most of us, usually need to be led to see the beauty and power of figurative language and to be coached on how to use it in their writing. I often referred to the activities I used to help bring about this awareness as the *training of their reading-writing ears.* The training regimen in my classroom included:

- Reading aloud and stopping frequently to point out a metaphor or brilliant image.
- Reciting poetry, "oohing" and "aahing" at its beauty.
- Passing out prose passages that exemplify figurative language.
- Presenting craft lessons and exercises on the use of literary devices.
- Showering classroom applause on students who use a literary device in their writing.

Along with this ongoing "ear training" program, each student also maintained a guide to figurative language called *"tools for literary touches,"* complete with definitions and examples. Students kept these guides in their writing folders and used them as references and reminders when they were writing or involved in author talks. I explained that literary devices were much like the finishing tools woodcarvers use to add the final touches to their creations. These touches make the difference between an ordinary carving and a piece of art, between a simple narrative and a polished story. What follows is an explanation of some of these tools.

Imagery

Written images found in stories provide a finishing polish that adds luster and brilliance to a description. Images appeal to our senses—

sight and hearing but also taste, touch, and smell. They make our writing like a camera that can move in for a close-up or back for a panorama. In writing about a young boy and his grandfather walking to a pond to feed the ducks ("Grandfather's Flight"), I said:

> Grandfather and I would walk through the crisp air of the early morning, yawning and dragging our feet through the grass, still stiff with frost.

I wanted to evoke how the world felt on that morning. "Yawning and dragging our feet," "crisp air" and "grass still stiff with frost" were images I chose to appeal to readers' senses. I could have written

> We walked to the pond.

but that would not have been as vivid. Later, in the same story, I *could* have written

> As we got closer to the pond, we could hear the water.

but I chose to say

> Getting closer to the pond, we could hear the water lightly gurgling and lapping on the shore, as the ducks dived beneath the surface for fish.

"Gurgling" and "lapping" are simple brushstrokes that suggest a sound as well as a feeling.

When I spoke to my students about imagery, I explained that we are all blessed with five senses, that our senses make us fully alive and our lives infinitely richer. We can watch dawn breaking on a quiet lake and view an unforgettable summer sunset. We can hear the impeccable fingerings of a fine guitarist. We can smell hot, fresh-baked bread. We can feel a sudden pang of affection or the pain of an injury. In our writing, we need to exploit our senses and convey with words what we want the reader to experience.

Imagery is best when it is embedded as inconspicuously as possible in description. Images serve to represent a particular thing or place or feeling. They not only *tell* they *evoke;* they not only describe they allow the reader to experience what the writer describes. I told children not to "tell" the reader that something was soft but to use words, details, and images that flaunt softness. For example:

African violet
baby's bottom
goose down comforter

well-loved sweater
clean, fresh bed sheets
feathery snowflakes
dandelion puff

I stressed that no matter what the overall success of a piece might be, it was well worth their effort if they were able to incorporate include one or two successful images.

Once they had examined sensory descriptions by many authors during craft lessons, I would have the class "go in their minds" to a place they could describe. "Notice everything you can about what you see—the sounds, the smells, the feeling you have being there—and write about that place through those perceptions." Later, children would read these descriptions aloud to the class. As another way of focusing on imagery, students used a story triggering sheet (see p. 60), to list as many sensory details as possible. In the story I wrote about my walks to the pond with my grandfather, I tried to recall as many images as I could before I wrote:

THE POND

crisp, cool air
stiff grass
scary trees—seemed like giants' arms
discarded lunch sacks
scattered newspapers
gurgling water
pastel sky

GRANDFATHER

quiet man
heavy eyebrows
never said much
splotchy hands
spoke to me through my mother
got excited seeing the ducks
saying "that one's yours"

Having brainstormed as many details as possible, I then tried to use them selectively as I wrote. The image of the giants' arms went in like this:

With my head nuzzled in the wool collar
of my jacket, only allowing me to peer around,

the trees seemed like dark and awesome giants,
stretching the shadow of their arms across our path
and watching our every step.

Used skillfully, imagery enhances a writer's thoughts. And, as Lucy McCormick Calkins states so well in her workshops, "Magical writing is contagious in the classroom."

Metaphor

Metaphor, broadly defined, is a relationship of implied or stated similarity between two things. Metaphors work not through specific description but through comparison. When Edna St. Vincent Millay wrote that a "wind with a wolf's head howled about our door," she conveyed the sound and feel of the wind by suggesting that it blew like a howling wolf.

When I spoke to my students about metaphors, I pointed out that they used them in their spoken language every day without even realizing it. For example, one morning when I was grouchy, one of my sixth graders described me as a "bear coming out of hibernation." Even though we use metaphors freely in speech, in writing we must select our comparisons carefully. If I describe fog as a "blanket" I am evoking a completely different image than Carl Sandburg's "little cat feet" from his poem, "Fog."

In writing workshops, I tell children to train their eyes to notice similarities: Who or what is this person like? What can that object be compared to? How might that experience be expressed as a metaphor? Aristotle stated that metaphors come from an "eye for resemblances." I suggest that students "seek out the unseen, the undersides of leaves," that they let their writing minds discover what makes dissimilar things alike. How is a sudden embarrassment like a startled flock of geese, or how is the ruffled hair we face each morning when we get up like the top of a yucca cactus?

In a craft lesson we would experiment with *like lines,* lines that showed how dissimilar things could be connected. We would write down five significant things, such as:

death
family
babies
siblings
murder

and try to connect them with ordinary things:

nail clippers
dogs
highway
chair
shoes

Here's a sample of some of our "like lines":

• Death and chairs are alike—they both take care of an end.
• Families are like highways. They're always going on.
• Babies and new shoes both have clean fresh "souls."
• Siblings are like dogs—you're always cleaning up after them.

and my favorite,

• Murder and nail clippers both take something away.

Continuing with a similar craft lesson exercise, we would choose topics and do a free-write using only similes. One such exercise with fourth-graders focused on body parts:

• My hair is like sea moss.
• My fingers are like leeches.
• My eyes are like emeralds sparkling in white snow.
• My hair is like waves in the sea.
• My eyeballs are like spots of oil in water.
• My hair is like corn silk, yellow and chocolate brown.

Another similar exercise involved experimenting with metaphors to express emotions:

• My joy is a squeak of delight.
• When I'm lonely, I'm invisible as a ghost.
• When I'm dumbfounded, I'm a disarranged jigsaw puzzle.
• My sadnesses are tears that never quit.
• My unhappiness is a bag of tears ready to burst.

Another craft lesson exercise explored the way objects could be personified. Using *tree* as an example, a group of third-graders wrote:

*The branches waved at
    the passing people.
Its roots dug their fingers
    into the earth.
The leaves shimmered
    with delight in the bright
sunshine.*

The trunk stubbornly braced
  itself against the wind.
The tree stood proud and
  erect.
The tree wears a shield of
  bark.

Metaphor, simile, and personification add depth and resonance
to a story. They round out our descriptions; they help us to sand
down the rough edges of a narrative, to chisel out a striking point.
They speak to readers through their imaginations. Metaphoric language separates a successful writer from a master writer.

Sound Play

Skilled writers use words in ways that cater to the value of their
sounds. When these devices are found sprinkled tastefully in a piece
of writing, they bring a spirit to the page and a liveliness to the
words. Alliteration, assonance, and onomatopoeia add to the
power—and the delight—of writing. In describing an angel de-
scending toward earth in her story *"Once a Good Man,"*

  the wind feathering her wings

Jane Yolen was conscious of the fact that the *alliteration* (repetition
of initial consonant sounds) of the "w" sound of "wind" and "wing"
would lift the sentence off the page and make it memorable to the
ear. By using such a quiet, subtle stroke she highlighted a beautiful
image. Later in the story she employed the same technique when
she wrote

  Instead of *f*lames and *f*ire,
  Instead of *m*ud and *m*ire,

and again,

  Instead of *c*louds and *c*hoirs,
  Instead of *r*obes and *r*ainbows.

Like alliteration, *assonance* (repetition of vowel sounds) calls attention to a writer's words. Unobtrusively, like shading in a painting,
Yolen repeats the "ur" vowel sound (turn, turning, churning) in this
passage from her story "The Wind Cap":

  He saw neither the turn of the seasons
  nor the turning of the soil. Nothing but
  the churning of the waves.

Another popular kind of sound play is *onomatopoeia*. An author selects a word or words that imitate a sound. The word "hiss," for example, imitates the sound a snake would make, as does the word "splash" for the sound of someone diving into a pool. The word "splat" clearly imitates the sound of a spoonful of Jell-O hitting the floor. In the story-poem "The Cremation of Sam McGee," Robert Service uses the word "sizzle" to convey what poor old Sam must have sounded like frying in the boiler room. When used selectively and with surgical precision, onomatopoeia can often strike a humorous chord.

In the classroom, I had my students experiment with the sound values of words using *word tinkering* exercises (also referred to in *When You've Made It Your Own... Teaching Poetry to Young People*). One of these activities involved a plastic bag filled with hundreds of individual words on strips of paper. Children reached in and took a handful. Spreading them out on the floor, they began to "tinker" with various combinations, not necessarily meaningful combinations but those that sounded good to their ears. I advised them, "Look for combinations of words that startle you because of the interesting sounds they create." Here is a sampling of some of their word-tinkering discoveries:

Curling blue-silver butterfly wings.
Jagged laughing muscles.
Ancient silver snakes shudder.
Swaying musical blossoms.
Flopping spray files.
Invisible muzzled monkeys.
Violent giddy dimples.
Twilight misty-forest wishes.
Twinkle tasting snowflakes.
Foggy creep moon.

Tinkering with words in this fashion forced students to shift their focus from meaning to sound value. The exercises gave them practice in what I like to call "messing about with words." "From time to time," I told them,

> *when you are working on a story, pull back from what you are trying to say and "mess about" with the words of a sentence or passage. Shift them around, add different words, play with their sounds, and see if you discover something you like.*

I am sure I would never have come up with this passage in "The Fiddler from Victor," if I had not been willing to "mess about" with my words when the barkeeper from Cripple Creek first encountered the skeleton of Aaron Kelly:

> Why, that Barkeep' just sat and stared—his jaw locked open in a frozen scream. Then he starts a-shakin' from the floor up. First, his toes start tap-tingling underneath him. Then, his knees began knob-knobbing together. His ribs start ring-rattling behind his vest and his hands a-shakin' like the leaves of a "Quaky" tree.

Periodically, as a craft lesson to review the "tools," the children and I would take a story, pull out an example of an author's figurative language, and examine it to see if we could determine what made it so effective. In Isaac Bashevis Singer's story, "Zlateh the Goat," students discovered some fine word-tooling:

> . . . wind wailed, first with one voice, then with many.
> . . . sound of devilish laughter.
> . . . so quiet in the hay that his ears rang in the stillness.
> . . . the moon shone, casting silvery nets on the snow.
> . . . white, quiet, dreaming dreams of heavenly splendor.
> . . . the moon swam in the sky as in a sea.

Each week, I would select a sentence, a phrase, or some other example from students' writing for what we called a *Literary Touch Award* (see Figure 4–7). Sometimes we put these excerpts, attrac-

Figure 4–7 Literary Touch Award

tively written out in calligraphy, up on the bulletin board. Because of these awards, children's enthusiasm for figurative language became infectious. As they grew increasingly familiar with this kind of language and confident about using it, they were transformed both as readers and writers. As readers, they enjoyed and appreciated words more. Their reading tastes expanded as they became increasingly attuned to an author's use of literary devices. At the same time, they became less tolerant of "ho-hum" writing. As writers, they set their sights higher; they demanded more of their words as well as their writing selves. They learned that reading is more than reading—it is being delighted by words.

A WRITER ALONGSIDE YOUR STUDENTS

The last section of this chapter is in the nature of a demonstration. I have selected three different genres of stories: the personal narrative, the adapted or retold folktale, and what I refer to as the enchantment tale. With each of these, I have demonstrated from my own writing how they may be used in a classroom to explore different stylistic avenues of writing. With the personal narrative, we have the opportunity to practice with effective setting description and explore a writer's point of view. With the adapted folktale, we gain an insight into a highly structured and repetitive story form. We also see how regionality and/or ethnicity can be used in a story. The enchantment tale affords the students a chance to work with the fairy tale/quest motif and to try their hands at a highly romantic or embellished use of language.

I have chosen to use my own stories in this section—not because I have any illusions about their extraordinary literary value. Much finer examples of each story genre are easy to find. I do, however, know my own thoughts and processes better than those of any other writer. If students learn best through the demonstration process, as I believe they do, then I am confident I can best explain and illuminate my own processes to them. I can demonstrate firsthand, from my own efforts, instead of describing another author's work from a distance. Finally, by using my own writing, I can practice what I preach in my workshops: "Be a writer, alongside your students."

"Rememories"

In my storytelling I often use a short poem that echoes an ancient African story opening as a lead in to the personal narrative stories I call "rememories."

Rememories—
Let them come,
Let them go,
For they are the treasures
  of your soul.

I wish I could lay claim to the coining of this delightful word, *rememories*. In fairness, however, I must give credit where it is due. Once in a writer's workshop I was explaining to my sixth graders that we would be writing about events from our own lives, "things that we remember from our pasts." I had asked, "What do we call those things we remember?" In one of those not-so-rare, wonderful moments created by a serendipitous sixth-grade tangle of the tongue, a bright-eyed girl raised her hand and blurted out: "Rememories."

What the girl did not realize was that she had discovered the perfect term for the type of writing we were attempting. We were not writing down memories or actual remembrances; those demand a factual account. The term *rememories* suggests instead a "revisit" to a memory, recasting and possibly reshaping events from our own recollections in the form of a story. In so doing, we are, as Lucy McCormick Calkins states, "reclaiming" the experience for ourselves. The one steadfast rule I stressed in writing rememories was "Never let the actuality of the event get in the way of the truth of the happening." Constructing stories from memories allows writers to manipulate reality by recasting events in the shape of a story. More important, it affords students the opportunity to value and validate the significant moments of their lives, the events they cared about.

In my classroom, I maintained what was called a "rememory bag"—a plastic bag full of individual story starters that might trigger a rememory:

- One of my favorite family traditions is . . .
- One of the most beautiful things I ever saw was . . .
- The hardest lesson I ever had to learn was . . .
- As a young child, my favorite day of the week was . . .
- My best family time is . . .
- I remember my first day at school as . . .
- My favorite spot in the whole world is . . .
- A day I'd like to relive is . . .
- My most painful experience was . . .
- One mistake I'd love to correct would be . . .

- The best advice I ever received was . . .
- A special possession I have is . . .
- One of my pets that I remember the most vividly is . . .
- A time I felt the most alone was . . .
- A teacher I remember the most is . . .

I introduced rememories in two parts. First, the children and I would examine a number of published personal narratives and discuss how each author presented his or her story. Then we would exchange our own verbal "rememories." As a warm-up exercise, each student would reach into the rememory bag and select a story starter; he or she would ponder it for a moment and then from the story stool recount a quick rememory. Our shared stories functioned much like a group brainstorming session, since each one reminded the rest of us of many of our own memories.

We would then have a craft lesson to walk through the process I followed in writing one of my own rememories. I used "Grandfather's Flight" referred to earlier, which centers around a small boy, his aging grandfather, and their weekly walks. In the story, the grandfather wakes the boy each Sunday morning to accompany him to the pond to feed the ducks that live there. At the turning point in the story, the boy innocently asks his grandfather if the ducks would miss them if they didn't come to feed them every Sunday. As the boy recalls:

> He looked down at me, his eyes for the first time losing their sparkle and appearing so sad and vacant that I felt they could look right through me. It frightened me. He turned his head toward the flock of waterfowl. They were skirting the horizon at the far end of the pond in brownish ripples of down-stroking wings. "They'd be all right without us, I suppose," I heard him say but in a voice I'd never heard before. "See . . . they nearly paint the sky with their wings as they leave."

At the end of the story the grandfather dies, and the boy imagines that his passage to heaven is like the flight of the mergansers they had watched each week at the pond:

> I wondered if Grandfather was in heaven now looking down through the pale skies at Mom and me. I bet he was. I bet he went there like his magnificent mergansers in flight—with his head and body perfectly level not looking back for one moment, his arms and hands extended like wings in smooth up and down strokes gliding him closer and closer to heaven—

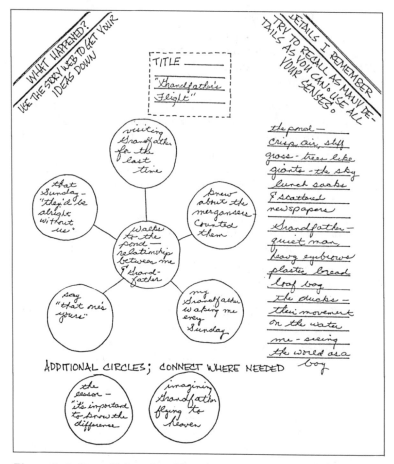

TITLE _____

"Grandfather's Flight"

WHAT HAPPENED?
USE THE STORY WEB TO GET YOUR
IDEAS DOWN

DETAILS I REMEMBER
TRY TO RECALL AS MANY DE-
TAILS AS YOU CAN. USE ALL
YOUR SENSES.

visiting
Grandfather
for the
last
time

that
Sunday —
"they'd be
alright
without
us."

drew
about the
mergansers.
Counted
them

Walk
to the
pond —
relationship
between me
& Grand-
father

say
"that one's
yours."

my
Grandfather
waking me
every
Sunday

the pond —
crisp air, stiff
grass — trees like
giants — the sky
lunch sacks
& scattered
newspapers
Grandfather —
quiet man,
heavy eyebrows
plastic bread
loaf bag
the ducks —
their movement
on the water
me — seeing
the world as a
boy

ADDITIONAL CIRCLES; CONNECT WHERE NEEDED

the
lesson —
"it's important
to know the
difference"

imagining
Grandfather
flying to
heaven

Figure 4–8 Story Triggering Sheet for ''Grandfather's Flight''

until he could barely be seen except as a tiny bright speck far
off in the early morning colors of the sky.

After I read the story to the class, we would look at how I used a
story triggering sheet to help me think of ideas (see Figure 4–8). I
would then show them an illustrated process sheet for my writing
of ''Grandfather's Flight'' (see Figure 4–9).

I told the children that writing is truly an act of faith; first, that
we have something to say, and second, that we can find the words
to say it. I also mentioned a few additional key ideas:

Figure 4–9 Illustrated Process Sheet for ''Grandfather's Flight''

Not all personal events necessarily develop successfully as a story—choose one that begs from inside you to be told as a story.

When you tell your story and struggle to get your ideas on paper, imagine a ''friendly audience''—one that will always enjoy what you have to say. As you write, imagine that you are simply ''telling'' your story to a friend.

Always remember that written language can create an illusion of spoken language—as if the writer were talking to you—so pull back frequently and listen to what you write.

As the children began developing and writing their own rememo-ries, we had two additional craft lessons, one on *setting* (where does the story take place?) and another on *point of view* (who is narrating the story?) In considering setting, I asked, "How does the writer make readers feel as if they were right there where the story was happening?" Using "Grandfather's Flight" I pointed out some of the ways I tried to convey a vivid sense of the story's setting:

> The park benches would always be empty this time of morning, except for an occasional ruffled newspaper or crumpled-up brown lunch sack.
>
> . . . as if the sun had—ever so slowly—pulled back the night curtains, allowing in the colors of the morning.

"Does the writing make you feel as if you are actually there?" I asked them. "What words help create that feeling? What tools for literary touches did I use?" I also talked about how details can create a sense of a close-up camera shot, helping readers *see* with the same clarity as the writer. "Description is a willing and on-call servant of the writer," I told them, "so call upon him frequently." Here are two passages from the story I pulled out to illustrate this point:

> Sitting there, we watched as a line of mergansers pattered on the water surface momentarily, then, with a great flush of activity, lifted themselves up, leveling off in a swift and direct formation, and began flying toward the open sky. We could hear their familiar "karring" in the distance.

> I went to Grandfather's room to see him. He looked very weak. His face was pale like the sky sometimes looked in the morning right before the sun would reach over the tops of the trees and light the pond. His lips seemed dry and crusted with little white balls of spit. He spoke very slowly.

The author's point of view is another important consideration in writing a rememory. To talk about point of view I used the illustra-tion of an automobile accident at a busy corner. Everyone who sees the accident describes it differently. Someone who sees it from a high window overlooking the corner might describe it quite differ-ently from someone who sees it from a distance behind, on the street. The same is true with stories. My grandfather might have described our weekly walks to the pond very differently than I did. I am sure my mother had yet another, different view.

I explained that there are two general points of view: *first person,* in which the story is told through the eyes of one of the characters, and *omniscient,* in which the story is told in the third person and the narrator-writer knows every detail, feeling, and thought of each of the characters. As a craft lesson, we would take a story such as Tomie de Paola's *Now One Foot, Now the Other* and sketch out the author's options. In the story, a grandfather (Bob) teaches his grandson (Bobby) how to walk by holding his grandson's hands over his head to help him balance and saying, "Now one foot, now the other." When the grandfather has a stroke, it is the grandson's turn to teach his grandfather to walk again during his recovery. Standing in front of the grandfather so he can balance himself, by holding onto the boy's shoulder, the grandson repeats the phrase, "Now one foot, now the other." We made a chart comparing the author's point-of-view options (see Figure 4–10).

We also looked at a number of stories written from different points of view, and we returned to my story as an example of a first-person point of view.

> I never knew when he first began walking to the lake every Sunday to feed the ducks. I guessed that it was after Mother had given up trying to force him into accompanying her to church. There were just the three of us living together then, and Grandfather was a stubborn man whose age, Mom said, had enhanced his stubbornness even more.

> Lying in bed that night, I kept staring up at the ceiling knowing that my grandfather wasn't in the room above me, wasn't in his bed, but seeing him anyway. I could see the crusted spit on his lips and the way the color had been drawn from his face the last time I saw him. I remember how wrinkled and splotchy his fingers had looked. I wondered what it was like to die. Did you feel anything? Did you close your eyes and fade away like they sometimes did in the movies?

Through the process of learning about, experimenting with, and eventually writing a rememory, children came to know firsthand that different kinds of story require different kinds of skill. They also discovered that they themselves were a deep pool of story material, that their lives were rich in detail and significant incident. By seeing moments of their lives through the focus of their writing minds, they brought into clearer view the truth of those times.

Point of View		
Omniscient	First Person	
The narrator would know:	*Bob (the grandfather) would know:*	*Bobby (the grandson) would know:*
• The relationship between Bob and Bobby.	• His teaching Bobby to walk.	• How he felt about his grandfather.
• How each character feels toward the other.	• How he would play with Bobby.	• What he remembers from his times with his grandfather in his younger years.
• How each character experienced the stroke – how each reacted.	• Bobby's first words.	
	•·Bobby's efforts in teaching him to walk.	• The information his parents gave him regarding his grandfather's stroke.
• Who did what, when.	• His eventual recovery.	• His fear around his recovering grandfather.
• The details of the stroke.	*What he would not know:*	
• Bobby's parents' concerns with Bobby during the crisis.	• How Bobby felt at school when he was in the hospital.	*What he would not know:*
• What came before the time of the story.	• How Bobby reacted (away from him) after he returned home.	• How he learned his first word.
• How things eventually turned out after the end of the story.	• What Bobby felt and thought when he couldn't talk as a result of the stroke.	• Medical issues surrounding his grandfather's stroke.
	• How Bobby remembered the phrase to help him walk.	• His grandfather's thoughts during the stroke and recovery.
		• His grandfather's reactions to Bobby when he could not talk or move.

Figure 4–10 Point-of-View Options

In the Folk Tradition

Modern writers who choose to adapt folktales or to use themes from folk tradition have more material to work with than they can possibly absorb in a lifetime. (Joseph Campbell's remarkable life and work might be the only exception!) My own library contains easily five thousand individual folk stories. In his monumental study of the folktale, Stith Thompson identified over twenty-five hundred types of folk stories. Multiply each of those types by the many motif variations and then again by the endless versions from around the world ("Cinderella," for example, has over three hundred versions), and it is clear that our ancestral "foretellers" have left more than enough stories to inspire young writers.

It is beyond the scope of this book to discuss the extensive scholarship about folktales—interested readers may want to refer to the list of recommended readings. In a classroom setting, however, I found that a few general facts about folk tradition and folk literature were useful. Here are some of the general ideas I mentioned to my students:

- Originally traditional folktales were not written down but passed orally from generation to generation.
- Folktales exist in many versions. Many stories have migrated from one culture to another.
- In the simple folktale world, realism takes a back seat to the likes of enchantment, magic, and fantasy.
- Personal characteristics such as persistence, virtue, cleverness, and courage bring desirable rewards to the folktale characters who possess them.
- Villainous characters oftentimes meet a violent, but clearly deserved, demise. The violence is never gratuitous, and it occurs swiftly and in context.
- Most folktales end on a positive note, often illustrating that high aspirations and noble spirits prevail.

Of all story forms, folktales are the most predictable. Because they were transmitted orally, they have been honed by their tellers into easily remembered units, often structured in groups of three (three wishes, three daughters, three gifts), since the more simply and predictably a story is structured, the easier it is to remember. Many folktales (again, because they were first spoken and remembered, not written) also rely on a recurring element—a line, an event, or even a variation on an episode that is repeated throughout the story—for example, "Not by the hair of my chinny chin chin." Think of a folktale you heard or read years ago; you will probably be able to recall a repeating element even though you may have forgotten many details. Repetition often acts like a trumpet blare announcing a folktale. Finally, folktales reflect the regional culture or ethnic background of the teller. In the English version of "Jack and the Beanstalk," for example, Jack steals the giant's golden eggs, goose, and harp. In "Jack and the Bean Tree," an American version from Appalachia, on the other hand, Jack steals the giant's rifle-gun, skinnin' knife, and coverlid (bedspread). When we tried adapting tales, my students and I directed our attention to these three folktale characteristics: simple folk structure; repeating element; and regional flavoring.

In a craft lesson, I walked students through "The Fiddler from Victor," my adaptation of the old story of "Aaron Kelly's Bones." I read aloud the original story from Alvin Schwartz's book, *Scary Stories to Tell in the Dark*. It is a retelling of one found along the South Carolina coast before 1940 (Schwartz credits the collection of the tale to John Bennett, under the title "David Aaron II" in *The Doctor to the Dead*). Here is a summary of the story:

> Aaron Kelly died and was buried, but that night he gets out of his coffin and comes home, finding his family sitting around the fireplace. He asks, "What's going on?" They try to convince Aaron that he is dead, but he refuses to go back to the grave. He just sits in front of the fire, rocking and warming his hands. One night, a fiddler comes to court the widow (since Aaron is dead). When the fiddler begins to play, Aaron can't help himself; he starts dancing, and his bones start dropping off—all except his bald head bone, which just grins, saying "Ain't we having fun?" Finally, the family gathers up all the bones, mixes them up (so Aaron can't put them back together), and returns him to the ground, where he stays.

In my adaptation, I set the story in Cripple Creek, Colorado, a couple hours' drive from the school, before the turn of the century, when it was a thriving, gold mining town. The children were quite familiar with Cripple Creek and knew some of its lore. Aaron Kelly and his wife Jessica live in a small cabin just outside of town. Jessica is described as one of the most attractive women in the area; Aaron is well-known for his practical jokes and pranks. After each prank, Aaron is known to repeat the same words: "Ain't this fun?" As in the original version, Aaron dies and is buried on a hill in back of their cabin. After a particularly bitter Colorado winter, he returns to the cabin as a skeleton and refuses to leave. He just sits, rocking back and forth in a rocking chair,

> . . . creakin' and crackin' and grinnin', and rubbin' his hand bones together in front of the fireplace.

When the first signs of spring arrive, so do the suitors to court the pretty Jessica. The first to arrive is Mike Foreman, a barkeeper from the local saloon, who is invited in by a not-sure-what-to-do Jessica and offered a glass of lemonade. Just as the lemonade glass reaches Mike Foreman's lips, the rocking chair (which appears to be empty and has its back to Mike) starts

> creakin' and crackin' and rockin' back and forth—on its own.
> Mike starts a'shakin' with that glass of lemonade rattlin' against his teeth.
> Soon that rocking chair starts to move itself around—creakin' and crackin'—until it's swung all the way around, and there sit the bare, bare bones of Aaron Kelly. Aaron just stares out of them empty eye sockets and grins. He slowly lifts up his arm bone and claps it—clickety-clack—on his leg. His jaw bone drops open: "Ain't this fun?"

Needless to say, Mike Foreman launches the lemonade glass into the air and leaves the cabin in a hasty fashion. The same scene recurs when Hank Williams, whose daddy owns the richest mine in town, comes to court Jessica. Finally, the fiddler from Victor arrives, and the events are repeated. But rather than throwing the lemonade glass, the fiddler asks Jessica if those bones like to dance.

> "Oh, yes," says Jessica. "Aaron did like to step out on occasion."

So the fiddler commences to play, slowly at first, then faster and faster, until Aaron's bones stand up and begin to dance. Soon the bones work themselves loose and begin to drop off, flying in every direction. This, of course, doesn't stop the dancing Aaron. He keeps dancing until his bald head bone comes slamming to the floor:

> "Ain't this fun?" he grins, as Jessica and the fiddler sweep up the bones into a burlap sack and redeposit them—mixed and stirred up real good—in the grave site.
> And do you know what? Why, that pretty, pretty Jessica, she done married the fiddler from Victor.

As this summary shows, I followed the traditional folk structure triad (three suitors and three episodes) in my adaptation. I also repeated the various elements in threes:

- Each of the three suitors calls on Jessica, is invited in, and is offered a glass of lemonade
- Each suitor brings the glass to his lips, and the rocking chair starts to creak and crack and swing around on its own

• Aaron Kelly says, "Ain't this fun?" three times.

By following the pattern of *three,* I was working in the folk tradition. But I also put my own fingerprint on the story: I set it in Cripple Creek hoping to give it another life. I encouraged students to do the same. All folk stories have been changed and adapted over time. The folk tradition is an ongoing one. When we work with folktales, we have the opportunity to embrace something that is older than recorded time and newer than the day before yesterday.

Another process I shared with children was how I went about giving the story a regional texture. First I read a few books about Cripple Creek, keeping a mental list of the bits and pieces of information I called regional "flavoring." As a fingering exercise before drafting the story, I brainstormed about Cripple Creek (see Figure 4–11). I could have used the same process, I told them, to place the story in modern, downtown Denver or in a logging camp in Oregon. In addition, I created what I hoped would be three true-to-life, turn-of-the-century characters. Again, I listed those characteristics my reading suggested might be typical:

MIKE FOREMAN	HANK WILLIAMS	THE FIDDLER FROM VICTOR
(barkeeper)	(son of wealthy gold mine owner)	(musician)
dusts off shirt	rents carriage	wears bib
puts on clean vest	arrives in waistcoat	overalls
slicks back hair	and derby hat	tucks fiddle
picks handful of	brings store-bought	under
wildflowers	bouquet of flowers	his arm
for Jessica		rides horse from
walks to		Victor to
Jessica's cabin		Cripple Creek

And I attempted to use colloquial speech to complement the actions and appearance of the characters. Here are some snatches of the dialogue:

"Now, Jessica, you know me. I'm Hank Williams and, well, my daddy owns the biggest mine here, and I've come to court you, if I may."

"Well, it be OK . . . why don't you come sit a spell here on the sittin' sofa?"

And later,

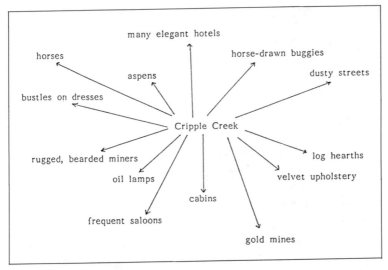

Figure 4–11 Brainstorming Web

"Now, Aaron, I loved ya dearly, but you is dead! Dead and properly buried, and you just gotta stay in the ground."

In writing dialogue, writers try to capture an approximation of speech. No one in stories talks the way people do in "real life." Dialogue is an illusion of conversation, a technique for revealing the character's nature through speech. Colloquial speech combined with regional details gave my story the texture of what I call "rocking chair prose," a vernacular style that creates the "sense of a story being told." This was the same effect I wanted students to achieve in the tales they wrote.

My intermediate students participated in a variety of activities that focused on folktales. The object of these activities (aside from exposing the students to many different folktales) was to have them see how chameleonlike folktales really are—how the same basic story can show up in different dress in various geographic regions and cultures, and to have them discover that "Lazy Jack," "Jack and the King's Girl," and "Epaminondas" are all variants of the same story.

In examining different versions of stories, we composed comparison charts delineating the similarities and differences between various versions. Here are some of the criteria we used in our analysis:

- main character(s)
- setting
- cause of lowly position
- type of cruel treatment (if any)
- element of magic (if any)
- villain
- number of episodes
- problem of story
- tasks that characters must perform
- agent of help for main character
- means of accomplishment
- solution to problem
- outcome for villain
- outcome for hero/heroine

Individual students also designed game questions for individual folktales, mimicking the television game show "Jeopardy." Here is an example for the tale of "Lazy Jack." The student who wrote the game questions would read,

The answer is "confusticated."
What is the question?

and then he or she would call on the first person who had the answer.

How Jack felt following his mother's directions each day.

The game would continue:

The answer is butter.
What is the question?
[What did Jack put on top of his head?]
The answer is best dirty breeches.
What is the question?
[What did Jack wear every day?]
The answer is "Jack, Jack, Jack, Jaaaack!"
What is the question?
[What did Jack's mother scream every day he returned?]
The answer is long, skinny rope.
What is the question?
[What did Jack tie around the roast to walk it home?]
The answer is "Gonna git to marry her!"
What is the question?
[What was the rich man's promise?]

In the end, the enduring folktales have much to offer writing students. In the predictable folktale structure, children have a clearly designed story model. Unlike pattern or formula books that only require the insertion of a word or two, a folktale adaptation demands that students study another culture or time. The vernacular writing style of the folktale insists that students train their ear to the sound of spoken language and attempt to recreate it on the printed page. During their exploratory work with folktales, recurring motifs, thematic similarities, and cultural variants become a working part of their literary repertoires. These insights and skills will serve children as both writers and readers in the years ahead.

Enchantment Tales

I want to present one last story type to illustrate how different genres may be used in the classroom writing workshop. It is more commonly known as a fairy tale, but I refer to it as an enchantment tale. I use the term *enchantment* because it seems to describe the basic dynamic of such stories more accurately than the conventional label. A still better term, one used by folklorists to describe stories such as "Cinderella" or "Snow White," is the German word *Märchen,* but there is no English equivalent.

Regardless of what we call them, enchantment tales rely on familiar motifs (castles, deep forests, kings, queens, princesses, princes). In these tales, the main characters are human beings, frequently good, humble sorts who overpower adversaries, gain kingdoms, and marry the desirable princes or princesses whose affections they have earned. Folktale scholars note that, although characters in fairy tales vary greatly in appearance, age, occupation, and rank, they generally perform several standard actions in the course of the plot. Here are a few typical actions found in fairy tales:

- A misfortune or need is made known; the hero or heroine is approached with a request or command; he or she is then sent to go on a mission.
- The hero or heroine is allowed to leave home in search of personal fortune.
- The hero or heroine acquires a magical agent and uses the agent to gain his or her fortune.
- A difficult task is proposed to the hero or heroine. Several (usually three) attempts are required to attain success.
- Through the course of a story, the hero or heroine is given a new

Enchantment Tale Plots

a(n)	poor small humble powerless honorable fair kind unselfish loving	hero heroine	goes on a quest violates a forbidden order is given a task is sent on a mission attempts to gain leaves home in search desires
of for	fortune revenge fame a magical agent recognition	and along the way	tricks encounters fights defeats deceives overpowers
a(n)	witch ogre villain troll giant	and is recognized but is victorious and	receives rightful recognition gains maturity marries a princess or prince ascends to the throne lives happily ever after receives great wealth

Figure 4–12 Enchantment Tale Plot Sheet

appearance and proceeds unrecognized. (Norton 1983, 203)

Various patterns or combinations of these actions appear in all fairy tales. A simple plot model I have used with youngsters in one of my beginning writing workshops is shown in Figure 4–12.

Using this model as a story starter, children can create a variety of plot lines:

An *unselfish* and *loving heroine leaves home in search* of a *magical agent,* and along the way *defeats* a *witch* and *marries a prince.*

A *poor, honorable hero goes on a quest* for *fortune* and along the way *encounters* an *ogre but is victorious* and *ascends to the throne.*

When they used this enchantment tale plot sheet students would read their plot to a friend, who would be allowed to ask three questions. Thinking out and answering the questions would help the writer focus on some of the details of the tale. For example, a student wrote:

A humble hero is given a task for revenge and along the way tricks a witch and is victorious and receives rightful recognition.

The partner asked (and he answered):

- What was the task? To destroy an evil witch and free her slaves/servants.
- How did he trick the witch? By digging a pit and deceiving and tricking her into falling in.
- What was his right recognition? He received the king's daughter as a bride and half the kingdom to rule.

As predictable and stylized as fairy tale plots are, their characters are even more stylized. Princesses are not merely well-mannered, they are "unparalleled in goodness and sweetness of temper" (as Perrault describes Cinderella). Villains are not just occasionally wicked, they are the essence of evil. To demonstrate their natures, enchantment tale characters rely on exaggerated or symbolic action. Heroes do not simply express mild flutters of infatuation when they meet their beloved; they immediately profess their undying love and propose. Jealous stepmothers display their evil natures toward children not by withholding dessert but by ordering them killed.

Through their archetypal use of black-and-white characters in stylized plots, enchantment tales serve as a stage for the symbolic enactment of larger human concerns: the value of loyalty versus betrayal, of courage versus cowardice, the eventual outcome of honorable or unselfish behavior, the consequences of personal greed or laziness.

The recognizable motifs and content of these tales create what Max Luthi, in his book *Once upon a Time*, calls a "literary style." This distinctive style became the focus of the writer's workshop. When we wrote our own enchantment tales, we attended to these stylistic elements:

- Romantic or embellished language.
- Flat, black-and-white characters.
- A plot line based on a quest or journey.

To illustrate these elements I told the class an enchantment tale of my own, "Land Where No Light Ever Reached." Summarized briefly, it is the story of two sons, identical twins, who were given different gifts by a fairy on the day of their birth.

To the first son, christened with the name Boldare, the fairy graciously bestowed all the powers of the animal kingdom.

"You, Boldare, shall have the endurance of a mountain goat, the speed of a deer in flight, and the strength of a wild bear."

To the second son, to whom the name Timond was given, the fairy granted all the powers of the flowering kingdom.

"Timond," the fairy said, "shall know and possess all that the forest is. The sky, trees, foliage and wind shall be at his call."

As it so happened, the sons lived in a kingdom that had been ravaged by a giant who dwelt in the "deepest bowels" of the forest. During the night, he would emerge and sneak into the kingdom in search of food. The first-born daughter of the kingdom's wealthy king had been carried off by this giant. So grieved was the king by her loss, he proclaimed that whoever could destroy this giant would receive his younger daughter as his bride and the kingdom to rule with her.

Upon hearing this, Boldare, whose powers were like those of the animals, ignored his parents' warnings and charged into the forest. Unfortunately, his brash, headstrong nature ensured his failure at the hands of the fierce giant. Then Timond, whose gift it was to know the ways of the forest, was sent in search of his brother.

As Timond traveled down the mountain toward the forest, the trees nodded. The branches swayed, stirring a gentle breeze. In accordance with his gift from the fairy, he had come to know the magic of the forest. As he walked, the tree roots that had so confused the way for his brother gently released their hold on the earth and formed an arch to make a passage for him.

Timond, of course, used what he knew to overpower the giant and free not only his brother but also the missing princess.

When the king saw his older daughter, so overcome with joy was he that he threw open the gates of the castle so that all could come and admire the beauty of the two princesses. A great banquet was held, and the king, true to his promise, gave his daughters in marriage—the younger daughter to Timond and the older one to Boldare. The two brothers and their wives then ruled the kingdom together for many, many years, with both wisdom and strength.

I showed my students how I worked to achieve a romantic, embellished style. Here, for example, is how Boldare speaks:

"Then, indeed, only I, Boldare, am capable of overpowering this great giant and winning the hand of the beautiful princess."

and

"That, old man, is quite simple," said Boldare. "The giant's death at my hands promises great fortune and a beautiful princess."

Does anyone really talk like that? Not in *my* circle of friends. But in the world of enchantment tales, such language evokes the courtly aura of the timeless world. Here is how I described the king's younger daughter:

So stunning was this daughter's beauty that, it was said, upon arising in the morning, the first smile that floated out from her lips dispersed the clouds of morning mist that hung over the mountain peaks. The emerald valleys shimmered at the sight of her.

And here is a description of the old man both Boldare and Timond encounter on their journey:

Seated before the hut was an old man as withered and wrinkled as a thousand years of worry. His white beard hung down to his knees, and he seemed to hunch over from the very weight of it.

In a craft lesson I explained that such romantic fairy tale language helps to suggest a fantasy world distant in time and place. We do not say "he stood tall," we embellish the idea; "he towered in the sky like a lonely pillar." We do not simply state "the forest was dark," we elaborate:

The forests surrounding the valley were so dense with tangled branches and leaves that in places hardly a thread of golden sunlight could pass through.

The telltale brush strokes of romantic language are stylized, ste-

reotypical words and phrases to which our ears become so accus-
tomed as we read or hear fairy tales. Here are some examples from
my story:

    once upon a time
    bestowed a gift
    deserving newborn
    know and possess
    embracing
    cherished land
    plundered by this giant
    a procession was made
    a proclamation was passed
    without any further ado
    royal duties
    subjects
    befallen
    rejoiced
    summoned
    overcome with joy
    great festive banquet

Along with its lofty language, my enchantment tale also portrays
black-and-white characters. The king is wealthy and all-powerful,
as all proper fairy tale kings should be. His daughters are without
equal in beauty. The giant is an unrepentant monster who ravages
the kingdom.

Finally, true to the genre, the plot involves a quest or journey.
On a literal level, the journey involves a descent into the land where
no light ever reached and a safe return. Many of my classes have
drawn a story journey map to illustrate the movement from the
brothers' mountain-top home down into the darkness of the giant's
forest and then out into the daylight of the royal kingdom. On a
symbolic level, the story reveals what are really two sides of an
individual's emerging identity as he searches for completeness,
overcomes adversity, and eventually integrates his divergent natures
into a mature personality. Boldare must learn that it is not through
strength alone that one succeeds, and Timond must learn that he
can venture out by using and trusting the abilities he has. The lesson
is one for all of us: we mature and succeed by merging both wisdom
and our strength.

Students' success in writing enchantment tales is directly related
to their exposure to this literary style. My students reread a variety
of fairy tales, looking at them with the eyes of a writer to observe

how the language was embellished and how the symbolic nature of the characters was revealed. Figure 4–13 shows an independent study sheet for fairy tales that I hoped would help students better

Figure 4–13 Independent Study Sheet for Enchantment Tales

ENCHANTMENT TALES

1. Title of book

_____

2. Name of fairy tale

_____

3. Name of the hero or heroine

_____

4. Who or what is the villain?

_____

5. Descriptive words you associate with three of the tale's characters (tasteful slang acceptable)

Name of character: _____   _____   _____

Descriptive words: _____   _____   _____

_____   _____   _____

_____   _____   _____

_____   _____   _____

_____   _____   _____

On Your Own Paper

6. Can you locate examples of home-rooted language, fairy tale style, in the story? Are any examples of poetic language used in the story?

7. If a verbal agreement is made in the story, describe it and explain what happens as a result of the breaking or keeping of the agreement.

8. What is the climax of the story?

9. Can you design a story journey map for the story?

10. Describe in detail the setting of the story. Include illustrations if you want to.

11. Identify a major problem faced by one of the characters.

12. How is the problem solved?

13. Creative thinking: How might the problem be solved other than how it is solved in the story?

understand their nature and style. By using these sheets with individual fairy tales and discussing their discoveries within their reading groups, students begin to see, for example, that Tattercoats, like Cinderella, is a "neglected, beautiful, sweet, lovely golden-haired" heroine. Or that the witch in "Rapunzel" is wicked, pitiless, and hateful like so many other fairy tale villains. From their reading they also gathered and recorded many examples of fairy tale language. Here is an example from Jacobs's version of "Tattercoats":

> The grandfather sat looking out the window. He wept great tears, until his white hair and beard grew down over his shoulders and twined around his chair. It crept into the chinks of the floor, and shears were needed to cut him loose.

The graduate students in my university language arts classes have developed a number of individual learning guides and activities for each of the fairy tales they use in their classroom teaching. Here are some questions for "Beauty and the Beast" and "Rumpelstiltskin" used by Margaret Zimbrick, who teaches fourth grade.

BEAUTY AND THE BEAST

1. *React* to the statement, "Beauty is only skin deep."
2. What do you think is beautiful?
3. Explain this quote: "It is only with the heart that one sees rightly, what is essential is invisible to the eye."
4. What qualities do you find most *admirable* in people? Make a list and *rank* them in order of importance to you.
5. In the tale "Beauty and the Beast," Beauty is homesick for her family. Have you ever been homesick? Describe your experience. What did you do to overcome your homesickness?
6. Pretend you are a counselor at a little kids' camp. You are preparing new counselors to work with new campers who will probably experience homesickness. What advice will you give them to help them deal with this problem?
7. What makes the beast beautiful?

RUMPELSTILTSKIN

1. Who is the villain in this story?
2. Interview six classmates who have read "Rumpelstiltskin." Ask them who they think is the villain. Record their responses.
3. Is it possible that this story has more than one villain? If so, who are they? Explain your answer.

4. From the information given in the story, compile a list of character traits that describe the following:

The king
The miller
The daughter
Rumpelstiltskin

5. Make a chart showing the positive and negative characteristics of each character.
6. In the tale, the poor miller lies to the king about his daughter. His daughter *also* lies to the king by taking credit for spinning straw into gold. What would *you* do if you were expected to perform a task that was beyond your *capabilities?* (You may want to give an example from your own life—something you have done.)
7. *React* to this statement: "It's OK to tell a little white lie." Fully explain your answer.
8. Why does Rumpelstiltskin not accept a substitute for the miller's daughter's child? Explain.

Different versions of traditional enchantment tales can provide an ideal subject for classroom discussion. The many versions of Cinderella stories serve as a good example. Children can compare Andrew Lang's "Cinderella," Joseph Jacobs's "Tattercoats," and the native American version collected by Frank H. Cushing, entitled "The Poor Turkey Girl" for their similarities and differences. I often asked students to make comparison charts according to the different elements of the fairy tale (setting, characters, problem, magic, promise or agreement, final outcome). With the Cinderella stories, for example, students filled in information about the use of magic:

	CINDERELLA	TATTERCOATS	THE POOR TURKEY GIRL
MAGIC	Used magic wand to change pumpkin into carriage, mice into horses, rat into coachman, and lizards into footmen.	Herdboy plays his pipe and Tattercoats' rags were transformed to shining robes; the geese were changed to pages.	Gobbler pecked and strutted and changed rags to a white mantle.

While they explored variants of different stories, my students also enjoyed reading and writing parodies. Roald Dahl's delightful book, *Revolting Rhymes,* has rhyming story-poem parodies of not only "Cinderella" but also "Snow White and the Seven Dwarfs" and others. Jane Yolen has written a parody of "Sleeping Beauty" entitled *Sleeping Ugly.* Add to these Babette Cole's *Prince Cinder* and Bernice Myer's *Sidney Rella and the Glass Sneaker* and children will have ample inspiration to write warehouses full of wild and wonderful parodies.

Many additional learning activities for use with enchantment tales can be found in *Once upon a Time: Creative Problem-Solving through Fairy Tales* by Jerry D. Flack. I will conclude here with a final activity of my own, "Chef Denman's World Famous, Timeless Recipe for Enchantment Tales" (Figure 4–14).

SUMMARIZING THE USE OF DIFFERENT GENRES

The "rememory," adapted folktale, and enchantment tale are examples of three different types of stories that have served well in the writer's workshop. I have by no means exhausted the classroom teaching possibilities for each genre, nor are these the only story forms available. Teachers might also want to look at fables, myths, fantasy, realistic fiction and many other genres. What I have hoped to demonstrate is a model for using different genres in the writer's workshop. The key idea here is "different." Different genres require different writing focuses, different prewriting activities, and distinctly different craft lessons.

In their lesson plans for a writing class, student teachers under my supervision sometimes say, "The students will write a story." "What kind of story?" I would ask, "and what kind of things does a story like that give you the opportunity to teach? What writing strategies will the students need in order to be successful?" Merely saying, "Write a story," implies that personal narrative is the same as folktale, that an informational story is exactly like a fantasy. Our students, particularly our intermediate through middle school writers, deserve more enriched instruction.

Writer's workshops may succeed in encouraging children to write, but they can be deficient in the attention they give to story genres. Too often, workshops fall short in three areas:

1. *Demonstration of the specific processes writers use when working in a particular genre.* We tend to homogenize the story-

CHEF DENMAN'S WORLD FAMOUS, TIMELESS RECIPE FOR
ENCHANTMENT TALES
Necessary Ingredients

One or two settings. For best results, use traditional one-sentence,
"bare bones" settings, such as "long ago in a far off land," or "in a deep
forest," or "in a great palace by the sea."

Two to five characters. Look for flat, black-and-white characters who
are not going to change on you during your story. Characters that are
either exceedingly bad or obnoxiously good and innocent are highly
recommended. It's also recommended that you have at least one bad
character and one good character to give additional taste to your tale.
You may look for an ogre or a witch to spice things up a bit.

One problem or task. Generally speaking, human problems—loyalty
versus betrayal, or courage versus cowardice, or even honor versus
greed—work best. A traditional task such as the defeat of a giant or the
discovery of a magic object, gives enchantment tales the most authentic flavor.

Optional Ingredients *(to be used at the writer's/cook's discretion)*

Magic. For an interesting twist to your tale, add a few elements of
magic. Transformations, spells, and magical agents are great. Or how
about some magical power or superhuman abilities? Use violence
sparingly.

Promise. A promise, broken or fulfilled, can be the ultimate touch in
an enchantment tale. Include the right amount of suspense around a
promise, and you have an award-winning dish.

Procedure

Take your setting and make it into a lead sentence. Mix in your characters. Add whatever other ingredients you decide to use (magic and/
or a promise) and set aside. Embellish freely with romantic language.
While the setting and characters are marinating, set your problem to
boiling. When the problem is bubbling, quickly mix it in with the setting and characters. Then let the story happen. What will the characters
do? How will they succeed? Watch as the hero or heroine attempts to
remedy the situation. How many chances will he or she get? For best
results, allow only three attempts. Finally, cover the dish and bake.
Clean up any leftovers and see if things turn out happily ever after.

Figure 4–14 Recipe for Enchantment Tales

writing process into one step-by-step procedure. In reality, the process varies from genre to genre. I encourage teachers to experiment whenever possible with the genre at hand, alongside their students. They can show student writers their own rough drafts and explain what "fingering" strategies they used. In author talks, they can share what worked and what did not work for them. And they can gear their instruction and presentations around what they themselves learned. Teachers can also talk about how other writers have gone about writing in a particular genre.

2. *Tie-ins to literature.* Reading and writing are frequently treated like arguing children in our classrooms: they are exiled to different corners. Yet reading and writing are inseparable collaborators in the writing process. Why do you think authors are photographed in their studies among cluttered stacks of books? Young writers need models for inspiration and guidance. Teachers who include reading of a particular genre while the students are beginning to write in that genre see their students' work taking on greater strength and proficiency. My rule of thumb is the greater the exposure to appropriate models, the better the writing.

3. *Instruction on the specific writing demands of different genres.* Different types of stories require attention to different writing issues. Point of view is important in personal narrative, and embellished language marks an enchantment tale; while colloquial dialogue can be just the flavoring necessary for an adaptation of a folktale. Teachers need to develop and use craft lessons that are appropriate to the writing concerns of the genre their students are working in.

In my work with teachers over the past few years, we have collaborated in designing lesson plans for writer's workshops that address these deficiencies. For each genre, we brainstormed and then mapped out our instruction in the following areas:

1. *Written concerns.* What is unique about how language is used in this genre? What makes this language usage different from that in other genres? How might the difference be demonstrated? What writing issues must writers consider? In what areas will they need to focus their attention?

2. *Craft lessons.* What specific craft lessons will be needed? How can I tie the craft lessons in with areas we have already examined?

3. *Organizational strategies.* How does a writer go about working in this genre? What strategies are useful? How would the writing process vary from that used in another genre? What insider's tips might help the beginner?
4. *Reading and writing activities.* What models from literature best exemplify this genre? What do we hope the students will discover about this genre? What types of activities will teach children about the specifics of this genre?

Figure 4–15 is an overall lesson plan that highlights and summarizes the activities I found most useful in introducing children to rememories, folktales, and enchantment tales.

Figure 4–15 Lesson Plan Sheet for Different Story Genres

Genre	Written concerns	Craft lessons	Organizational (fingering) strategies	Reading/writing activities
Rememories (personal narratives)	• creation of "story" out of personal happenings • point-of-view • setting	• use of believable point-of-view • setting portrayal • use of details	• rememory bag • story triggering sheet • story sequence sheet	• examination of different personal narrative stories • "process" presentation of "Grandfather's Flight" • writing own rememories
Adaptations of folktales	• folk structure of story: magic three and repetition of elements • regional/cultural flavoring • colloquial language	• "rocking chair prose" • use of colloquial dialogue • character portrayal	• hanging mobile • rising/falling action model • regional/cultural brainstorming and research	• comparison studies of different versions of stories • writing adaptation of tale with regional/cultural twist
Enchantment tales	• romantic language • use of common fairy tale motifs and symbols • creation of black-and-white characters	• embellishment of language with use of hyperbole • examination of black-and-white characters	• story sequence sheet • story journey map • fairy tale action plot line	• study of fairy tale motifs • examination of symbolic nature of characters • story journey map of different quest tales • writing of original tales • exploring parodies of fairy tales

A final word. To inspire young story writers, I tell them, as I often tell myself:

- Find your own pathways as a writer.
- Cater to what fascinates and obsesses you.
- Be on the lookout for stories, poems, and memorable excursions into language.
- Remember that all that you write will be yours—your recorded legacy—so honor your thoughts with your best efforts.

END THOUGHTS

TOUCHSTONE OF LITERACY

As I write, I am seated at my desk. On the wall directly in front of me are three pictures that have kept a watchful eye over my writing for many years. The first is a poignant black and white National Geographic photograph of an African storyteller. A circle of adults and children huddles close around him. The storyteller's hands are raised in a dramatic gesture, and his audience seems utterly absorbed in the story. Alongside the African storyteller is another picture, a detailed pen-and-ink drawing of a turn-of-the-century orator. A distinguished figure in an old-fashioned waistcoat and bow tie, he has the undivided attention of about a dozen people seated comfortably on the ground around him. They seem to be weighing every word as they listen. The third picture is a newspaper photograph of me telling a story to a group of youngsters. From the position of my hand and the look on my face, I suspect that Lazy Jack has just foolishly slapped a chunk of butter on his head to carry home to his mother. The smiling faces of the children have been caught in that moment just before they realize the butter is going to melt during Jack's walk home. The photo holds the promise of the laughter that is about to erupt.

These pictures, each from a different time and place, illustrate what I believe to be the true touchstone of learning. If you suppose that I mean stories and storytellers, look closer. Look at the faces in the audience. Feel as comfortable as the third grader stretched out on the floor, oblivious to those around him as he listens to "Lazy Jack." Sense the friendship of the two African girls sitting near the tribal storyteller. Forget whatever might need to be done around the house and be as moved as the members of the orator's audience. In each of these pictures, people of all ages are engaged in one act—the act of listening. *Listening* is the touchstone of all learning. As Jane Yolen suggests, humans "shaped and were shaped by the oral tradition. . . . The person," she writes, "who did not listen well, who was tone deaf to the universe, was soon dead" (Yolen 1981, 46).

Long before we learn to read or write, we listen: in our parents' arms, under the covers before falling asleep, around the dinner table in conversation, or in a corner of the classroom. Listeners are unbeknownst, incidental learners. Through the stories they hear, children develop an astute sense of cause and effect, and consequence. They rehearse problem-solving strategies and construct and revise hypotheses, all within the context of story. They experience the full range of human feeling by hearing stories and develop the conceptual and emotional tools they need to making sense of the world around them. But most important, as the writer Margaret Atwood has remarked, "From listening to the stories of others, we learn to tell our own." Listening acts as a catalyst for the eventual discovery of all that is valuable in language. It beckons us with the inherent promise of a lifetime of pleasure through words.

Unfortunately, not everyone realizes this promise. Contemporary society has strayed from the familiar pathway of oral language best epitomized by the storyteller. The mass media, in particular television and film, have replaced listening with viewing. Children today spend hours in front of the television set, which caters to an attention span of only a few minutes and usurps children's innate image-making capacity. As a result, the experience of a slower-paced world rich with incident and meaning, which is presented in spoken stories and poetry, is absent from many of our children's lives. Their listening minds, so naturally receptive to the satisfactions of spoken language, are under constant siege by the visual—the seductive, rapid-fire images of television and movies. Perhaps Bruno Bettelheim expresses the problem most clearly: "Television captures the imagination, but does not free it. A good book at once stimulates and frees the mind."

Many educated people today find little joy in language in comparison with the immediacy of visual media. Language in their minds is equate with rules of grammar or exercises in composition. Their experience of story is one of a dreaded reading assignment not of listening intently to a wonderful storyteller. As Robert

MacNeil, one of the creators of the television series, "The Story of English," and coauthor of the companion book, suggests, our "minds may no longer be adequately programmed for the pleasure" of language. "I think the society," he says, "is not listening enough. . . . The more I think about my own pleasure in the language and where it came from, the more I am convinced that it sprang first from *hearing* words and phrases, hearing poems and stories read aloud, and having heard them many times, keeping them clear in my mind's ear." (MacNeil 1988, 19).

MacNeil's listening experience as a child, and later as a student, is what all children should be able to expect of their world—not only at school but also at home. We learn to listen by being spoken to, by hearing stories, jingles, and rhymes, by being read to. Over time, the listening experience sets the stage for all the language learning that follows. The authors of *Becoming a Nation of Readers* state unequivocally that the "single most important activity for building the knowledge required for eventual success in reading is reading aloud to a child" (Anderson et al. 1985, 23). Listening acts as both the foundation and the ongoing support structure for literacy and learning.

Rediscovering the practice of listening ought to be the mandate—as well as the hope—of all parents and teachers truly concerned about the imaginative lives of children and about our society's literacy. Never has a solution to a problem been so accessible, so easy, and so pleasurable. To reinstill the habit of listening, we simply say, "Push away your books and pencils for a moment, children, and come gather around me. There's something I'd like to share with you." Then, let the time-honored magic of language work: "Once upon a time. . . . " Frequent and joyous use of "once upon a time" in our classrooms requires no governmental task force, no legislated curricular policy change. It neither needs to be supported by a bond initiative nor implemented with new textbooks, scope and sequence guides, or teacher inservicing. It takes only a teacher, a group of children, and a good book, and its value has historical precedent older than recorded time. "From the beginning," Sigmund Freud stated, "words and magic have been connected."

Children who regularly hear stories and poems don't know (or care, I suspect) about the educational advantages of what they are doing. They simply enjoy the experience. Learning and pleasure become one, and the act of listening has made it possible. Perhaps a short poem I wrote a couple of years after I left the classroom best expresses my feelings. I wish all children could be among the lucky ones.

LUCKY IS THE CHILD
> *Lucky is the child*
> *who has a teacher*
> *who with a book*
> > *on a frayed carpet*
> > *in a corner of a classroom*
> > *on a succession of quietly unassuming mornings*
> > *surrounded simply by a circle*
> > *of listening eyes*
> > *and curious, contented faces,*
> *sets into motion*
> *the first joyous ripple*
> *of an ever broadening*
> *ever expanding series of*
> *encounters with the world of books.*
> > *Lucky is that child*
> > *standing at the edge of a sea*
> > *waiting to embark toward a life*
> > *of full and lasting literacy.*
> *Lucky is the child.*

RECOMMENDED READING

Stories and Storytelling

Arbuthnot, May Hill. *The Arbuthnot Anthology of Children's Literature*. New York: Scott, Foresman, 1976.

———. *Time for Fairy Tales: Old and New*. New York: Scott, Foresman, 1976.

Barton, Bob. *Tell Me Another*. Portsmouth, N.H.: Heinemann Educational Books, 1986.

Campbell, Joseph. *The Complete Grimm's Fairy Tales*. New York: Random House, 1944.

———. *Myths to Live by*. New York: Viking, 1972.

Cott, Jonathan. *Pipers at the Gates of Dawn*. New York: Random House, 1981.

Hearne, Betsy, and Marilyn Kaye, eds. *Celebrating Children's Books*. New York: Lothrop, Lee & Shepard Books, 1981.

Kieran, Egan. *Teaching as Storytelling*. Chicago: The University of Chicago Press, 1986.

Laubach, David C. *Introduction to Folklore*. Portsmouth, N.H.: Boynton/Cook, 1989.

Livo, Norma J., and Sandra A. Rietz. *Storytelling Activities*. Littleton, Colo.: Libraries Unlimited, 1987.

Lukens, Rebecca J. *A Critical Handbook of Children's Literature*. New York: Scott, Foresman, 1976.

MacNeil, Robert. *Wordstruck*. New York: Viking, 1989.

Pellowski, Anne. *The World of Storytelling*. New York: R. R. Bowker, 1977.

Shedlock, Marie L. *The Art of the Storyteller*. New York: Dover, 1951.

Stillman, Peter R. *Introduction to Myth*. Portsmouth, N.H.: Boynton/ Cook, 1977.

Yolen, Jane, ed. *Favorite Folktales from Around the World*. New York: Random House, 1986.

Language Arts

Bosma, Bette. *Fairy Tales, Fables, Legends, and Myths*. New York: Teachers College Press, 1987.

Cullinan, Bernice E., ed. *Children's Literature in the Reading Program*. Newark, Del.: The International Reading Association, 1987.

Flack, Jerry D. *Once upon a Time: Creative Problem Solving through Fairy Tales*. East Aurora, N.Y.: D.O.K. Publishers, 1985.

Goodman, Ken. *What's Whole in Whole Language?* Portsmouth, N.H.: Heinemann Educational Books, 1986.

Hornsby, David, and Deborah Sukarna. *Read On: A Conference Approach to Reading*. Portsmouth, N.H.: Heinemann Educational Books, 1988.

Johnson, Terry D., and Daphne R. Louis. *Literacy Through Literature*. Portsmouth, N.H.: Heinemann Educational Books, 1988.

Luthi, Max. *Once upon a Time*. Bloomington: Indiana University Press, 1976.

Smith, Frank. *Insult to Intelligence*. Portsmouth, N.H.: Heinemann Educational Books, 1988.

Writing

Atwell, Nancie. *In the Middle: Writing, Reading, and Learning with Adolescents*. Portsmouth, N.H.: Boynton/Cook, 1987.

Bales, Paul Darcy. *Storycrafting*. Cincinnati: Writers Digest Books, 1984.

Calkins, Lucy McCormick. *Lessons from a Child*. Portsmouth, N.H.: Heinemann Educational Books, 1983.

————. *The Art of Teaching Writing*. Portsmouth, N.H.: Heinemann Educational Books, 1986.

Elbow, Peter. *Writing without Teachers*. Oxford: Oxford University Press, 1973.

Graves, Donald. *A Researcher Learns to Write*. Portsmouth, N.H.: Heinemann Educational Books, 1984.

————. *Writing: Teachers and Children at Work*. Portsmouth, N.H.: Heinemann Educational Books, 1983.

WORKS CITED

Anderson, Richard C. 1988. "Putting Reading Research into Practice." *Focus on Reading,* a special edition of *Instructor* (October).

Anderson, Richard C., et al. 1985. *Becoming a Nation of Readers: The Report of the Commission on Reading.* Champaign, Ill.: Center for the Study of Reading.

Bettelheim, Bruno. 1975. *The Uses of Enchantment: The Meaning and Importance of Fairy Tales.* New York: Random House.

Bettelheim, Bruno, and Karen Zelan. 1982. *On Learning to Read: The Child's Fascination with Meaning.* New York: Alfred A. Knopf.

Butler, Andrea, and Jan Turbill. 1987. *Towards a Reading-Writing Classroom.* Portsmouth, N.H.: Heinemann Educational Books.

Calkins, Lucy McCormick. 1986. *The Art of Teaching Writing.* Portsmouth, N.H.: Heinemann Educational Books.

Denman, Gregory A. 1988. *When You've Made It Your Own . . . Teaching Poetry to Young People.* Portsmouth, N.H.: Heinemann Educational Books.

———. 1986. "Storytelling Sticks, Ancient Semantic Maps." *The Colorado Communicator,* a publication of the Colorado Council of the International Reading Association (November).

Flack, Jerry D. 1985. *Once Upon a Time: Creative Problem-Solving Through Fairy Tales.* East Aurora, N.Y.: D.O.K. Publishers.

Fowler, Gerald L. 1982. "Developing Comprehension Skills through the Use of Story Frames." *Reading Teacher* (November).

Graves, Donald H. 1989. *Experiment with Fiction.* Portsmouth, N.H.: Heinemann Educational Books.

Hilton, James. 1978. "A Note on Story" in *Parabola.* New York: Society for the Study of Myth and Tradition.

Holdaway, Don. 1979. *The Foundations of Literacy*. Gosford, NSW, Australia: Ashton Scholastic.

————. 1987. *Independence in Reading*. Gosford, NSW, Australia: Ashton Scholastic.

Livo, Norma J., and Sandra A. Rietz. 1986. *Storytelling: Process and Practice*. Littleton, Colo.: Libraries Unlimited.

Luthi, Max. 1976. *Once Upon a Time*. Bloomington, IN: Indiana University Press.

MacNeil, Robert. 1988. "Listening to Our Language." *The English Journal* (October).

Martin, Bill Jr., and Peggy Brogan. 1972. *The Sounds of Language*. New York: Holt, Rinehart and Winston.

Murray, Donald. 1984. *Write to Learn*. New York: Holt, Rinehart and Winston.

INDEX

Instructional Strategies
and Activities

INDEX

Stories and Authors